THE LIFE AND HUMOR OF ROSIE O'DONNELL

THE LIFE AND

william morrow and company, inc. / new york

O'DON

HUMOR OF ROSIE

Gloria Goodman

O'DONNELL

[A BIOGRAPHY]

It is the policy of William Morrow and Company, Inc., and its imprints
and affiliates, recognizing the importance of preserving what has been
written, to print the books we publish on acid-free paper, and we exert our
best efforts to that end.

Library of Congress Cataloging-in-Publication Data

Goodman, Gloria
The life and humor of Rosie O'Donnell: a biography / by Gloria
Goodman.—1st ed.
p.   cm.
ISBN 0-688-15315-1
1. O'Donnell, Rosie.   2. Comedians—United States—
Biography.   Motion picture actors and actresses—United States—
Biography.   4. Television personalities—United States—Biography.   I.
Title.
PN2287.027G66   1998
792.7'028'092—dc21   98-2678
[B]   CIP

Printed in the United States of America

First Edition

1   2   3   4   5   6   7   8   9   10

BOOK DESIGN BY DEBBIE GLASSERMAN

www.williammorrow.com

CONTENTS

ONE

A Fan Is Born

The mother, in her early thirties, had black hair and blue eyes. Her little girl, about six, had brown eyes and dark brown hair. You would have known they were mother and daughter. Not only did they have similar rounded faces, but they both bubbled with laughter. The mother was taking her daughter to see *Funny Girl,* the movie version of the huge Broadway hit about Fanny Brice, the comic and singer who had been one of the great stars of the Ziegfeld Follies in its heyday after the First World War and into the 1930s. The movie marked the big screen debut of Barbra Streisand, the Brooklyn girl with the big nose and even bigger voice who had vaulted to stardom in the Brice role on Broadway. The mother and daughter who went to see the movie soon after it opened in 1968 were from Commack, Long Island, and they were both named Roseann O'Donnell.

The two Roseanns loved the movie. It was funny and it

was full of terrific Broadway songs by Jule Styne, and both mother and daughter liked anything with music and comedy. But this movie was something special for them both. The mother was an enormous fan of Barbra Streisand, and as soon as little Roseann had seen the movie, she announced that she wanted to grow up to be Barbra. Her mother suggested sweetly that Roseann didn't have quite that kind of singing voice. Her daughter replied, "I'll learn." Young Roseann soon learned all Barbra's songs from *Funny Girl*, and the ones from her record albums, too. "I'd go into the kitchen singing 'Second Hand Rose' with Barbra's accent," a grown-up Roseann, now known as Rosie and famous herself, would later remember, "and my mother would laugh and laugh. It was a great way to get attention, so I kept it up."

Roseann would also see her first live performance of a musical the year she was six, a production of *George M* at Long Island's Westbury Music Fair. Her mother would take her into New York to see a movie and the Rockettes at America's most glamorous movie palace, Radio City Music Hall. They would sit up in the third balcony, in the cheapest seats, eating lemon drops, looking down on the vast stage, where Rosie O'Donnell would hold forth herself nearly thirty years later, starring in her own comedy show on New Year's Eve 1995, and where she would host the nationally televised Tony Awards show in June 1997.

The little girl from Commack, Long Island, knew very early that she wanted to perform, wanted to be a star who made people laugh and sang songs for them. But the child, like her mother, was first and foremost a fan. In young Roseann's first ten years of life, at her mother's side, she became the sort of devoted admirer of movie and television stars, of singers and actors, who makes people with enough talent into stars. The critics can rave or rant about a star's given performance in a particular movie or show, but it is the fans that go to see them, no matter what, who make them stars in the first place. And little Roseann O'Donnell, like the mother for whom she was named, was that kind of fan. It was the fact that she started as such an avid fan that would eventually bring her a unique kind of success as a star in her own right, one who could talk to other stars in a way that the average person could completely understand and connect with.

The bond between the two Roseanns, mother and daughter, was particularly strong, but there were four other children in the O'Donnell family. Eddie was the oldest, followed by Danny, then Roseann, then sister Maureen, who was fifteen months younger than Roseann and shared her bedroom, and finally the youngest son, Timmy. Their father, Edward J. O'Donnell, had been born in Ireland but emigrated with his family to the United States when he was small. He was an engineer specializing in the development of cameras for spy satellites, and the family lived in Commack because it was near the Grumman airplane plant that was a mainstay of the Long Island economy. He made a good salary, but not the kind that went very far when you had five children, which meant not only cheap seats at Radio City Music Hall but, as Rosie O'Donnell has often noted, Hydrox cookies in the house instead of the more expensive Oreos. Their widowed grandmother, Kathryn Murtha, also lived with the family, helping her daughter with the five kids, but making for a very full house.

Commack was like many other Long Island communities an hour's drive or so along the Long Island Expressway from New York City: pleasant, middle class, and virtually indistinguishable from other towns in the area, having some older streets with larger homes from earlier times, but largely consisting of houses built in the post–World War II boom on Long Island. It was a nice, friendly place to grow up, and its proximity to New York City gave it a little more sophistication than such communities in the Midwest, say, but it was still a very middle-American kind of place.

People always seem to be surprised that somebody who grows up in a place like Commack can go on to become very famous, but they shouldn't be. Three of the greatest icons of the movies, Fred Astaire, Henry Fonda, and Marlon Brando, were all originally from Omaha, Nebraska. Talent will out, as the old saying goes. And young Roseann O'Donnell dreamed of being a star, a Barbra Streisand, Carol Burnett, or Lucille Ball, from a very early age. Even so, many people with talent never make it into the big time because they don't have the will, the drive, or the endurance to capitalize on their talents. Rosie O'Donnell herself has said that things might have been different if her mother hadn't died in 1973, when Rosie was ten.

Her mother was diagnosed with liver cancer in December 1972. The children weren't told what was wrong, but they knew that their mother was very ill—she was in and out of the hospital several times before dying on March 17, St. Patrick's Day, 1973. Rosie remembers being told only that her mother had "passed away." She wasn't even sure what that meant, and since the children weren't allowed to view their mother's body at the funeral home, or even attend the funeral, young Roseann sometimes wondered if she had just gone away because it was too much work having five children to take care of. At times she even fantasized that her mother was watching her when she was playing basketball, up there in the stands someplace, hidden from Rosie's view.

The loss of her mother was made worse by the fact that her father withdrew from the children, too. "Being a typically repressed and emotionally detached Irish Catholic family, we rarely discussed my mother's death," she told Patrick Pacheo in an interview in *Cosmopolitan* in June 1994. She later told Liz Smith, the columnist, that the family didn't even have many photos of her mother. "My father didn't keep a lot of stuff. In his effort to get over his own grief, he made some rash decisions about photos and things like that."

Her father did his work, but became less and less communicative, going out on weekends. "Every Sunday you could tell what happened on Saturday night. Because you'd hear . . . 'My name is MacNamara, I'm the leader of the Pack. . . .' He played the Clancy Brothers twenty-four hours a day. Sunday was Clancy Brothers day in our house." The children did their best to take up the slack in the household. Eddie (Edward Junior), the oldest, did a lot of the cooking, and Rosie found herself the organizer and peacekeeper in the family, young as she was. "I think that because there was a lack of guidance in the house," she has said, "I looked inside myself. Some kids fall apart in that situation and others become their own leader. I became my own leader and made rules for myself."

•   •   •

I think in my family everybody was funny. That's the way you were allowed to communicate. Typical Irish Catholic families, I think, you're not allowed to express your emotion, but if you catch the emotion in a joke you're allowed to express it.

Rosie O'Donnell to Conan O'Brien, 1996

•   •   •

Edward O'Donnell was not uncaring, even though he had great trouble expressing his emotions. The summer following his wife's death, he packed up all five children and took them to Ireland for a few weeks to meet their various relatives. In an October 1996 interview with *Irish America* magazine, Rosie recounted her memories of that trip. "I remember eating salt-and-vinegar potato chips and having sweets, the candy, those Marathon bars, remember those? We used to go to the woods and my cousin would shoot capguns and we'd hide in the bushes and watch the helicopters come because we were in Belfast for part of it. It's all sort of a fuzzy, hazy memory, but I do remember playing soccer all the time, which we never did in the U.S., and picking up the brogue right away and speaking that way for the whole time we were there and all my siblings making fun of me."

Back home in Commack, it was largely up to the children to keep the family operating. Their father "didn't have a clue how to do laundry," Rosie recalls, and his attempts at cooking were a disaster, including mashed potatoes that were pulverized before pouring off the water. When Rosie pointed out that the result was potato soup, not mashed potatoes, her father insisted that not only were they good, but that that was the way their mother had made them. Fortunately, their mother had taught each child how to make one different meal, and with that as a basis, they managed to get the family fed.

Still, their mother's absence was glaring, and it is hardly surprising that Rosie became deeply involved with television shows that featured families. Series like *The Waltons, The Brady Bunch,* and, later, *Eight Is Enough* gave the children, and Rosie in particular, fantasy families they could identify with. She watched with such concentration, and had such a good memory, that twenty-five years later she was repeatedly able to flabbergast guests on her talk show with details about the series they had starred in that they hardly remembered. "We were allowed to watch TV twenty-four hours a day," Rosie recalls. "And we did."

Despite all the time spent watching television, Rosie was

far too gregarious to turn into any kind of loner, and far too funny to have any problem making friends at school. She also gives a lot of credit to her teachers, who stepped in after her mother died to give her support and guidance. She is particularly grateful to her eighth-grade math teacher, whose name was Pat Maraval, and whom she would warmly introduce to the nation during the Commack high school reunion televised for her talk show. In interviews she had already paid tribute to Pat Maraval, saying: "She became a surrogate mom to me, she helped me to stay focused and feel loved, and I think she had the biggest effect on me. . . . She took me under her wing and helped me through all those adolescent girl things."

Young Roseann O'Donnell was not entirely a teacher's pet, however. She didn't study hard enough for that, and her attitude toward her elders was not always deferential. "I always felt I knew more than them. I got away with the attitude because I was funny." She vividly remembers how much her teachers in elementary school had liked her mother, who was very active in the PTA and for a while had been its president. When her mother came to the school, teachers would go out into the hall to talk with her. "They'd say to us, 'Read your books. We'll be right back.' There were glass windows along the hallway, and I remember my mom making all the teachers laugh." The daughter had the same gift, which stood her in good stead with both her teachers and her fellow students. But Rosie adds, "I was lucky I wasn't prone to getting into trouble. I was a kid prone to succeed."

She maintained a B average, more because she had such

a good memory than because she studied. And as she progressed through high school, she became the most popular girl in her class. She was elected senior class president, *and* homecoming queen, *and* prom queen. She wasn't the prettiest girl in her class (even then her weight went up and down), and she wasn't the best student, but interviews with her classmates over the years have always been dominated by the words "funny" and "nice," and many have said that the Rosie O'Donnell on the television screen five days a week is very recognizably the Roseann O'Donnell of Commack High.

. . .

Most of the kids in my class wanted to entertain each other, but my goal was to amuse the adults. I was the teacher's pet because I could make the teachers laugh.

Rosie O'Donnell in *Career World*, October 1994

. . .

During her school years Roseann made no secret of her ambitions to be in show business. "My career really started in school," Rosie has said, "because I did all the school plays and talent shows." That gave her a little experience, but it was not nearly as important as her trips into New York City to get standing-room tickets to Broadway shows. Sometimes this meant cutting classes, but with no mother to lay down any rules, and a father who wasn't paying attention much of the time, she got away with it. The money for these trips initially came from baby-sitting—former neighbors have said that Roseann sat for almost all the nearly thirty young kids in her immediate neighborhood. Occasionally, she has admitted, she also swiped money from her father's wallet to pay the train fare. Roseann was demonstrating real nerve, a characteristic kind that would serve her well in years to come, by going into Manhattan to catch a Broadway show on her own at such a young age. She was only thirteen, for example, in 1975, when she saw not only the musical *The Wiz,* which was geared to kids, but also Bette Midler's wild and sometimes risqué Broadway appearance in *Clams on the Half Shell.*

Bette Midler was immediately added to Roseann's pantheon of stars she wanted to emulate. "I didn't want to be like her," Rosie would say years later, "I wanted to be her." Of course, the program for *Clams on the Half Shell* was added to Roseann's growing collection of *Playbills,* which she often displays on her talk show. While Barbra Streisand remained a special heroine, there were more and more female stars of Broadway, movies, and television being added to Roseann's list of models: Florence Henderson, Lucille Ball, Carol Burnett, Mary Tyler Moore—all funny ladies.

In 1978, in her third year of high school, Roseann saw the new Broadway musical *They're Playing Our Song* by Marvin Hamlisch, who had already won a Tony for his score for *A Chorus Line* in 1976 and an Oscar for his score and title song for 1973's *The Way We Were* (starring Barbra Streisand, of course). The star of the show was Lucie Arnaz, daughter of Lucille Ball; and perhaps because Arnaz was still in her twenties, closer to Roseann's own age, the girl from Commack not only waited at the stage door to get Arnaz's autograph, but also began writing notes to her. By the late 1970s, the stars of the entertainment world were wary about replying to fan mail with anything but a signed photo or a printed note—there were too many cases of stars being harassed or even stalked by disturbed individuals. But Lucie Arnaz realized that Roseann was a wholesome if lonely young fan, and she actually replied to several of Roseann's notes, which gave both of them something to talk about when Arnaz appeared on her show in August 1996. Rosie still had the letters.

What Rosie wanted to be was an actress, but one night, when she was sixteen, she accepted a dare from some classmates and stood up to perform a comedy routine at a local restaurant, The Ground Round, which Rosie has described as basically a "McDonald's, only with waiters." And a bar, where area teenagers with fake I.D.s found it easy enough to buy a beer in those days. Rosie didn't have anything like an act, but this was "open mike" night, where the customers were given a chance to show off. If she wasn't really very funny, neither were the adults doing their thing, and she at least had the advantage of being very young, and cute in her way, and the customers, many of them men her father's age, cheered her on.

A more serious opportunity arose during her final year at Commack high school, 1979–1980. Rosie recalls: "We had

Senior Follies, which was sort of *Saturday Night Live* skits about the teachers." Young Roseann O'Donnell was, naturally, a star of this show. "I did Gilda Radner [of *Saturday Night Live*], Roseanne Rosanna-Dana, talking about school apathy, and I would impersonate her. And a local guy who owned a club in the area was a comic, and he asked if I would come and do stand-up in his club. I said, 'No, I'm going to be an actress.' He goes, 'Why don't you try it?' So I tried it. . . ."

This wasn't an open-mike amateur night thing. She was actually paid for her appearances, although the money wasn't any more than the $50 prize she'd won on a dare at The Ground Round. Still, she was getting paid for performing instead of baby-sitting or summer jobs at a T-shirt concession. The trouble was that she had no real act and found herself resorting to Don Rickles–style insults of the audience. "Where'd ya get that shirt?" she'd ask, and try to provide a funny answer. This kind of comedy is in fact treacherous and extremely difficult to pull off, and Roseann got away with it only because she looked like such a kid. But if no one got mad enough to attack back, nobody was laughing all that much, either.

Depressed about the whole deal, she made a classic amateur mistake. Having seen Jerry Seinfeld, then just making a real name for himself, on *The Merv Griffin Show,* she duplicated his routine at the club. The audience was not a group that watched daytime television; they were mostly working guys and their girlfriends, and they thought she was a scream. Success at last! But the other comics came up to her backstage, "real threatening like," wanting to know where she'd gotten such boffo material. When she told them, they let her have it. "When they told me I couldn't do that, that I had to do my own material, I was crushed, devastated. I mean, I didn't have any idea how to go home and make up my own jokes."

To the girl who wanted to be an actress, it was clear where the jokes came from—a writer had created them for a script that the actress then memorized. Write her own material? No way! But pride won out. If that was what they wanted, she'd show them she could do it. And gradually she learned. The Catholic school she'd attended when she was younger provided some material, which went over well with the predominantly Catholic audiences in the area (Rosie would later assert that she didn't even know anyone who wasn't Catholic until she went away to college). Her own Irish Catholic family was another source of humor, particularly her father and his annoying suspicions that she was smoking marijuana when she didn't even smoke cigarettes. These jokes about her father, in which she exaggerated both his Irishness and his stupidity, would serve her for years to come, and in an odd way are revealing of the fact that for all his "distance," he was paying enough attention to worry about his daughter's welfare.

Roseann O'Donnell began watching comedians on television more carefully, not to steal their jokes, but to observe how they used material from real life and turned it a little to give it a comic edge. Her act got steadily better. She was beginning to understand how to be a professional. But her father wanted her to go to college, and it made sense to her that a college education, especially if she could take a lot of courses in theater arts, could be helpful. She didn't have the kind of academic record that would get her into a top-ranked college, but she was smart enough and had a good enough memory to do well on entrance examinations. She certainly had a terrific record in terms of extracurricular activities and "school spirit," and colleges like to have some students who are strong in those nonacademic areas. For one thing, such leader types often go on to make more money than most of the academic stars, and help fill alumni coffers in later years.

So Roseann was accepted at a fine college: Dickinson, in Carlisle, Pennsylvania. It was one of the country's oldest institutions of higher education, having been founded in 1773, before the American Revolution. Now coeducational, it had a high teacher/student ratio and a diverse student body, which would expose Roseann to a much wider ethnic and racial mix than she had grown up with. Dickinson was a small college, with a student body of seventeen hundred, so she wouldn't feel overwhelmed, and it was located only about four hours from home in lovely country, just to the southwest of Pennsylvania's state capital of Harrisburg. Like many state capitals, Harrisburg is not a major city, but Philadelphia was only a two-hour bus ride away and a favorite weekend destination for Dickinson students.

Roseann worked in the administration office to help pay tuition under a work-study program that many students participated in, and she enjoyed both that and the college atmosphere. But she did not do well academically. In later years she would maintain that the students were "much smarter" than she was on the whole, but she was not being fair to herself. Rosie O'Donnell has proved again and again that she is as smart as they come. She simply wasn't academically inclined, which is a different thing. But she only managed a D- average her freshman year, which was not good enough to continue at Dickinson.

• • •

I always knew, since I was like four. I wanted to be Barbra Streisand. I wanted to be in Broadway shows. I was the only fourth grader who knew all the words to South Pacific. . . . *There was never a second choice for me—it was showbiz or nothing.*

Rosie O'Donnell in *Irish America* magazine, 1996

• • •

Never one to give up, however, she decided to try a much larger institution, Boston University, where some fourteen thousand students were enrolled. The city of Boston, and neighboring Cambridge, are home to Harvard, M.I.T., Boston College, and many specialized educational institutions in addition to Boston University, and the area is a major hub of amateur and professional theater activity. What's more, B.U. had a well-regarded theater school. Roseann auditioned, using material from the musical *Hello, Dolly!,* a huge Broadway hit starring Carol Channing and a host of successive actresses, including Pearl Bailey (as well as a movie that had starred her idol Barbra Streisand). Dolly Levi was a good role for Roseann's brassy persona, and she was given an acting scholarship to the university.

She loved all the theatrical activity in Boston, but her experience at B.U. would prove a bitter disappointment, and not especially because of the academic requirements. Instead, she was told off by an acting professor. "He told me the part of Rhoda Morgenstern had already been cast and that I would never make it as an actress." Since Rhoda, played by Valerie Harper on *The Mary Tyler Moore Show,* was a favorite character on a beloved show, it is quite possible that Rosie was putting too much Rhoda into her work in acting class. One of the problems with being a good mimic, as Roseann has always been, is that sometimes you do it without fully realizing it. At the same time, for every student any acting teacher has ever championed who went on to be a big star, there is always another one the teacher completely misses the boat on. The girl from Commack, Long Island, didn't realize that at the time, however, and his words cut deeply. Furious and humiliated, Roseann quit B.U. in February 1982. Years later, when she would appear in a very Rhoda-like role in the television sitcom *Gimme a Break,* Rosie would send that teacher a retaliatory note. But she had a long way to go before she was in a position to take that small revenge.

TWO

Stand-up Comic

Before leaving Boston, Roseann O'Donnell got her first professional job in show business. It came about by accident, and wasn't exactly a success. One night she talked her way into Boston's Comedy Connection by announcing that she was a comic from New York. She didn't even expect to get onstage, and didn't—at least not in Boston. The owners of the Boston club also had a place in Worcester, a working-class city in the middle of the state, forty miles inland. The club was called Plums. When a comic scheduled to appear there didn't show up, Paul Barkley of the Comedy Connection grabbed hold of the supposed "New York comic" named Roseann O'Donnell and bundled her into a car with the two performers who had shown up, Denis Leary and Steven Wright, and sent her off into the night. Leary and Wright, who would become stand-up stars long before Roseann, were also at the start of their careers, but they had a lot more experience than she did. Unprepared, Roseann bumbled through an improvised routine that failed to convince anyone that she'd ever be heard from again. However, everyone thought she was a nice girl, and she was paid the promised $60. In that sense, she was now a professional.

She had a great deal to learn, and she knew it. Returning to her father's house in Commack, she took a nine-to-five job at a nearby Sears, the only "desk job" she would ever have until she found herself behind another kind of desk on her own show in 1996. At night she pursued her dream of a show business career. She was popular as an emcee, thanks to her gift of gab and sheer likability, but she also began to really work on her stand-up skills at the Eastside Comedy Club in Huntington, Long Island, about fifteen miles from home. The club had been founded by Richie Minervini in 1979; by the time Roseann returned to Long Island, the acts at the club were being booked by Rick Messina, who would himself rise to national prominence as a booker. Rosie subsequently gave special credit to Minervini: "He gave me the breaks and took me under his wing. If it wasn't for him, I probably never would have done stand-up comedy." Messina played an important role, too, when he formed a group called The Laughter Company, which was to play on the usually dark Monday nights at the Eastside Comedy Club. The show was a mixture of stand-up and improv in the manner of Second City groups in Chicago and Toronto, with the improv section performed first, after which the five members of the group would conclude the evening with individual stand-up riffs.

While Roseann was not the strongest of the group at stand-up, she did have acting experience, even though it had been at the amateur level, and that was crucial in getting her into the group, since improv requires acting skills and the ability to mesh with other players in a skit. Some of the material was set, but half of it was improvised, and Roseann was good at that. In terms of her immediate future, it was the chance to work on her stand-up routine that would prove most valuable. Ultimately, of course, the experience in improv would be an asset on her television show; a quick uptake with guests, no matter what happens, is a major asset in a talk show host. Rosie is quite probably quicker at responding than anyone since Johnny Carson. It's a gift that not only gets laughs, but is invaluable in keeping the pace of a talk show lively.

Not that Roseann was thinking about becoming a talk show host in those days. She wanted to be an actress, but given her lack of credentials and serious training, stand-up seemed like a possible route—maybe the only one—toward an acting career. It was still a long shot. Today, one television show after another is being created around stand-up comics, but this was before Roseanne Barr, Dana Carvey, and Tim Allen had made the leap from stand-up to sitcom. In fact, they were out there getting started at the same time that Roseann O'Donnell was.

Even fifteen years earlier, stand-up comedy wouldn't have offered Roseann anything like the same opportunities. Vaudeville was dead, nightclubs had been hit hard by television, and television itself had only a few shows that brought unknown comic talents to the fore, including Lily Tomlin, Arte Johnson, and Goldie Hawn. In New York the Improv had started up in 1963, but Catch a Rising Star didn't open until the mid-1970s—and neither of the clubs paid its comics. There were a small number of local bars, like The Triple Inn in the West Fifties in Manhattan, that had talent showcases one slow night a week. Freddy Prinze showed up there occasionally before he suddenly rocketed to stardom, but such places were more interested in singers, nobody got paid, and it was extremely rare that an agent or booker went anywhere near them.

In Los Angeles the Comedy Store got going in 1972, and the L.A. Improv joined it in 1975. But it wasn't until a strike by comedians against the Comedy Store in 1979 that it, and subsequently other clubs, began paying the talent. By the early 1980s, as shown by Roseann's first professional gig at Plums in Worcester and by the very existence of the Eastside Comedy Club on Long Island, venues for stand-up comedy began to proliferate in a big way. In the first half of the 1980s, comedy clubs rose in number from less than a dozen to nearly three hundred. And they paid, some only a little, but an increasing number in the hundreds of dollars per week. For the first time since the death of vaudeville, it was possible for a comic to make a basic living by traveling around the country.

And so, after honing her skills for a while at the Eastside Comedy Club, Roseann hit the road. She doesn't recall the ensuing several years with much fondness. "You'd arrive in town and they'd have a kid come pick you up in a used

Vega or Toyota with a door that didn't close. You'd have to get in on the driver's side and climb over his lunch from Hardee's. All of us would be scrunched in the back seat, and he'd take us to this filthy condo where we would all live for a few days, with the sheets that have to be shaved because they had little bumps on them . . . rotten leftover takeout food in the fridge. Very disgusting."

Early on, Roseann O'Donnell was given a new name. When an emcee introduced her one night, the audience thought they heard the name Roseanne Rosanna-Danna, the signature character of Gilda Radner's repertoire on *Saturday Night Live.* Confused, and perhaps expecting to see Gilda, the audience booed. Who was this young woman anyway? The next time he introduced her, the emcee called her Rosie O'Donnell. The name stayed with her from then on, in part because it seemed to suit her personality better than Roseann.

Rosie, as she would henceforth be known, has professed admiration for Roseanne Barr, saying that she "paved the way for all of us. I think she is a wonderfully funny woman. She bravely and courageously uses her own life to help other people, and I have nothing but respect for that, but I would never do that." Nor did Rosie do the trash talk that Roseanne Barr, Whoopi Goldberg, and many other women comics made use of. That kind of act was taking the routines of predecessors such as Phyllis Diller and Joan Rivers and pushing the envelope further, adding a good deal of Lenny Bruce/George Carlin/Richard Pryor obscenity to the mix. Rosie doesn't put down such comics in any way, but it was never her style to talk dirty or to disparage other people. She didn't feel that the end justified the means when it came to putting people down, nor that "the fact that someone laughs justifies the hateful, hurtful comments that you make."

. . .

Kids are fun, but not fun to have physically. And I hate it when women lie to women without children about that. . . . "It's nothing, they put a little Vaseline on your thighs, the baby flies right out." The thing I hate most is when women say, "Yeah, it's painful, but it's the kind of pain you forget." I don't think so. I think if I passed a watermelon through my nostril, I'd remember the day.

Rosie O'Donnell, doing stand-up, 1986

. . .

This didn't mean that Rosie was a Goody Two-Shoes, or lacked the nerve to get tough when it was required. The comedy club circuit has always been rough, as all but the top nightclubs were in earlier days. People in the audience are drinking, and they can get nasty. Comics seem to draw out the worst in a certain kind of loudmouth who decides to show how funny he is. And if you are going to hold your own against hecklers, you have to come right back at them in the crude terms they can best understand. Rosie was perfectly capable of shutting such types up by saying, "The next time you come to a comedy club, stop at a drugstore, buy a condom, and put it over your head. If you act like a dick, you might as well dress like one."

But her actual routines didn't depend on dirty words, male bashing, or what is known in the comedy club world as "PMS jokes." As Rosie would say in 1988, "I make fun of what I know best. Growing up in a big family, learning not to hate your stepmother, dieting, listening to a four-year-old try to tell a joke—that kind of stuff." It was material that anyone could connect with. And it often gave her more of a chance to act than the routines of many comedians. The story of the four-year-old trying to tell a joke, for example, wasn't just a matter of getting to a punch line—in fact, there wasn't one. Instead, she was presenting a miniature skit, showing both the four-year-old in action and the reaction of the bemused adult. What was funny was the fact that the four-year-old *couldn't* tell the joke. And the humor was all in the telling of it, the showing of it. It's a truism that one person can tell a joke, and even the punch line isn't funny, while another person tells the same joke and has us laughing because of the way they tell it, long before the punch line is reached. This is a gift. Everyone in the comedy business, writers, performers, and club owners alike, will say that you can't teach people to be funny. Either they are or they aren't. They can get funnier as they gain experience, and learn to judge an audience. The polish of a top comic is won through hard work, and lessons learned over a long period, often for little money in dingy clubs. That's one reason why even a major star like Robin Williams will go to a club like the Comedy Store in L.A. to break in a new routine. The feedback from the audience helps the comic pace and fine-tune his jokes. But no amount of work can make an unfunny person funny.

Rosie O'Donnell was funny. She'd always been funny— at home, at school, wherever she was. At the beginning of her career, her act was unstructured and sometimes something of a mess. However, she almost never bombed completely, although she often felt that she had. "I tanked," she'll say to this day, remembering some awful night long ago. But numerous club owners have gone on record over the years to say that she never really tanked, that there were always laughs, and that even when she wasn't at her best, audiences *liked* her. Likability is a strange component in the acts of some comics. The persona of Jack Benny, for example, who was Johnny Carson's idol when he was growing up, was of a snooty tightwad. But people liked him even so. Later on, while Don Rickles made a major career out of being mean, he allowed something else to show through that people liked: He doesn't really mean it, they'd think, and laugh even harder at the next zinger. Other comics have played their likability for all it was worth—Carol Burnett being a classic example. Her acid portrait of Eunice, a thoroughly unlikable kind of person, wouldn't have worked if the audience didn't know Carol would be out there at the end of the show tugging at her ear in such an endearing, friendly way.

This does not mean that people who appear likable in

their acts are actually people you'd like to spend a weekend with. Some of America's most beloved performers are known for being anything but likable in real life. The public is aghast when someone like Bing Crosby, who was presented in an extremely unflattering light in his son Gary's book, is knocked off the pedestal. But the quality that other stars project onstage, in the movies, or on television is sometimes genuine. No one from Rosie's long years on the comedy club circuit has come forward to dispel the impression that she was a remarkably nice person in a difficult profession.

Rosie was famous for her willingness to sit by the door at a table following a show and sign autographs, sometimes hundreds of them, even after she had become much better known. She was also extremely pleasant to be around backstage, as many other comics, as well as club owners, have attested over the years. The affection shown toward her on her talk show by people she once worked with on the road, like Tim Allen, is clearly genuine. Sometimes, however, she had to win over the club owners. She said in 1996 that although there might be as many as six hundred women comics by that date, when she started out there were about six. That fact increased audience interest in women comics, but many club owners were initially quite suspicious of them. Rosie remembers one incident with special vividness. "You're the third woman we've had, and the first two sucked," a club owner said, and then added a kicker: "If you stink, we're not hiring any more." "That's a lot of pressure, isn't it?" Rosie asks rhetorically. "The responsibility of my entire gender ever performing there again? It was horrible."

There would be a lot of other horrible moments over the years, both onstage and off. George Mair and Anna Green, in *Rosie O'Donnell,* have quoted Rick Haas of the Chicago club Zanies on the problems confronting women comics before they even face an audience. "It's hard enough for a man to do this," he says. "A guy gets a booking at an out-of-town club. He drives by himself, maybe at night, to this club and parks in the dark parking lot, walks into a strange club, and does his show. That's hard enough for a guy. For a woman, that is a life-threatening situation."

In fact, Rosie herself has talked about being on edge on the road, sometimes even frightened. "The other comics were much older. They'd pick up women at the bars, bring them home, and have sex in the rooms next to mine. I was like twenty and totally freaked out from hearing these noises through the wall. I put the dresser up against the door. Everybody was doing drugs and drinking, and I was just this little girl on the road, scared in her room."

Even though she might sometimes be scared, Rosie was determined to make her mark, and to stay with the only route she could see to a major career in show business. Like many others, Rich Haas put his finger on the quality that makes the difference for any performer. "It takes drive. What sets Rosie O'Donnell apart? She's got that drive. Why is Rosie now the happeningest thing going, and Paula Poundstone is nowhere to be found? Drive." Ironically,

Paula Poundstone resurfaced in the fall of 1997—on Rosie's own show as a monthly correspondent going out with a video camera to interview real people.

Drive certainly is a vital ingredient in show business success. There's more to it than that. Paula Poundstone, for example, has her fans, and Jay Leno has used her talents, too. But she is almost always described in the press as "offbeat." This makes her something of an acquired taste. Rosie is someone who can connect easily with a mainstream audience. In her early days on the road, there were plenty of people to tell her that she would never make it. There were those who said she was too New York, or too heavy; there were some who thought she was too tough (for a woman) or not tough enough because she didn't do nasty putdowns of names in the news. Criticism didn't run off her like water off a duck's back by any means, and she found some of it hurtful, but in one sense it only made her more determined. At the Aspen Comedy Festival in 1996, she said, "Some women when I started out were jealous of other women. They thought, 'If she gets *The Tonight Show,* I can't.' My philosophy always was, 'If she did, we can, too.' Success breeds success."

This positive attitude, coupled with her drive, got Rosie through many difficult moments. She also avoided the temptation of trying to do material she wasn't comfortable with, trying to become different. After all, she'd grown up making mainstream people laugh—family and schoolmates and the people who went to the "hamburger joint" on Long Island called The Ground Round where she got some of her first bookings. There wasn't any place more mainstream than Long Island. If she could make those people laugh, there were bound to be a great many others she could reach. When she went on the road, she carried a notebook in which to jot down funny things she saw happening around her, at malls and fast-food restaurants, things that would tickle other mainstream people like herself. Her drive might be exceptional, but what she found funny was what anybody who had grown up in the suburbs across America would find funny. "I'm much more middle American than anybody ever realized," she has said, reacting to the astonishment of some people that her talk show would appeal to such a broad spectrum of the American middle class.

"Everything in my act, if it didn't happen to me, happened to my sister," Rosie notes. So she made people laugh about growing up in the suburbs. She made people laugh about growing up Catholic, always a rich vein of comedy if it is done with affection, as the success of the stage musical *Nunsense* across America has shown. She made people laugh about her father, with her perfect mimicry of his Irish brogue. And that appealed to people from a great many ethnic backgrounds whose parents or grandparents had come to America from other places and tried to cope with a different culture. However, Rosie's secret weapon was her almost uncanny knowledge of popular trivia, especially as it related to television.

A great many comics feel that they have to be right on top of the breaking news to make an impact. Of course that works, as Jay Leno and David Letterman and Johnny Carson have shown. Getting off a crack about the latest mess a president—any president—or any movie star has gotten into means that it will be repeated by people the next day around the watercooler, and if it's a good enough crack, it will get picked up by newspapers and magazines for their "quote of the day" fillers. Rosie has never done that, though. She understood that people's memories were deeply stocked with images and associations from the television they watched and the popular music they heard when they were growing up. And if you could plug into those memories with both affection and humor, you could do two things at once: You could make people laugh at the same time that you awakened nostalgia for the days of their youth.

You couldn't do that, however, just by mentioning a title, like *The Brady Bunch* or *The Partridge Family* or *Laverne and Shirley*. You had to mention a specific scene: "Remember when Laverne opened the door and there stood. . . ." Not only did Rosie remember all the scenes, she remembered the dialogue. The same was true with popular songs. Never mind quoting the opening line or the famous refrain of a song, she knew the whole damn thing. And audiences loved that. It brought back pleasurable moments they had half forgotten, or forgotten entirely. There was Rosie O'Donnell making them real again, and they could laugh with her about those memories the way they once laughed in the school lunchroom. All their yesterdays came flooding back. What fun! More than that, what bliss. Rosie made her audiences laugh, but she also made them feel good.

Rosie's funny stories about her father, focusing especially

on his encounters with modern technology, were also a hit. Audiences generally understand that when comics talk about their wives or parents in a show, a good deal of exaggeration is involved. In subsequent years, as the public learned more about Rosie's childhood and the fact that her father had been a rather distant figure after the death of Rosie's mother, interviewers began to ask questions about how he had reacted to her jokes about him. By then it was known that Edward O'Donnell was an electrical engineer by profession. Could he really have so many problems with an answering machine? Rosie said that her father was "not stupid," and admitted to some exaggeration. As for her act, which he had seen very few times live, and usually pretended he had not seen on television, she explained, "The jokes are done with love and he kind of likes it." She noted, however, that his comments were usually couched in the form of someone else's opinion. "He'll tell me, 'Mr. Ryan at work saw you on TV and thought you was very funny, luv.' " But by 1994 she had reached the point where she felt sure enough of herself to be more candid. "The father I have in the show is a lot nicer and a lot more approachable than the father I had in reality. My father in reality is not the affable Irish leprechaun." This is the opposite of comics whose "take my wife—please . . ." routines are often in contrast to a happy thirty-year marriage. Trust Rosie O'Donnell to find a way to be funny about her father that makes him nicer than the reality.

While Rosie increasingly went out on the road for appearances at the growing number of comedy clubs across the country, she was back on Long Island when the lucky break came that would propel her to a new level of recognition. In 1984, after a performance, a woman came up to her and asked how Rosie would like to be on *Star Search*. This was a new television show hosted by Ed McMahon, Johnny Carson's longtime cheery straight man on *The Tonight Show*. It was technically a show for amateurs, but Rosie knew about it, and it was becoming very popular. Apparently thinking she was being taken for a ride by the woman, Rosie gave a brusque "oh, sure" answer. She was embarrassed to discover that the question had been for real, and that the woman was McMahon's daughter Claudia, out scouting for her father.

Even while knowing that the offer to set up an audition was genuine, Rosie hesitated. Was this the right move for her? For one thing, she was a professional. That wouldn't matter in terms of getting on the program. She'd never been seen on television or even reached the point where she had been a headliner at a major club. So far as the show was concerned, she was an amateur, and many other contestants had similar backgrounds. But if she auditioned and didn't get on, or got on and bombed, and word got out about her failure, there was the possibility that the clubs on the comedy circuit would write her off. She had not spent the past two years on the road to be considered a has-been at twenty-two.

Still, if she succeeded to any degree on *Star Search*, it would give her a lot more visibility and make her more desirable to the comedy clubs. Audiences were always more receptive to comics who had television credits—you were a little ahead of the game with that sort of credential. She talked it over with friends and other comics she knew well. Some were against the whole idea, thinking she didn't stand a chance. Even at that early stage of the show's success, thousands of people, male and female vocalists, musical groups, and other performers, were being auditioned for the 160 yearly spots on the show, and there were only a few slots available for stand-up commedians.

Rosie was all too used to hearing people tell her she was wasting her time trying to have a show business career, and the fact that some were saying that about this opportunity probably had a lot to do with her decision to go ahead. You didn't tell Rosie she wasn't up to the competition without her feeling a rush of "I'll show them" determination. She did the required taped audition, passed muster, and flew out to California to appear on the show.

Amateur talent shows had a long history. In the heyday of radio, Major Bowes's show had been extremely popular; it featured many future stars, including an audience-pleasing moppet named Bubbles Silverman, who sang opera, of all things, and would later become much better known as the great American opera star Beverly Sills. Radio also had *Ted Mack's Family Hour,* which later had a run on television. The most successful of the TV shows was *Arthur Godfrey's Talent Scouts,* on the air from the late 1940s to the late 1950s, which introduced such future stars as Tony Bennett, Rosemary Clooney, and even Johnny Cash.

Yet there hadn't been an amateur hour in a quarter century when *Star Search* made its debut in the fall of 1983 as a syndicated program. It was possible for a top winner to earn as much as $100,000 on the show, but that meant surviving for many weeks and getting into the finals. In each category of competition, one week's winner, who would pick up $3,500 in prize money, would be pitted against a new challenger. There was less competition in the stand-up comedian category than in the ones for singers, but it was still tough.

Just as was true in the comedy clubs, female comedians were still something of a novelty, and Rosie herself was different from the usual woman comic. There was something about the combination of her kewpie-doll appearance and her New York accent that made her both unusual and appealing. She dispatched the previous winner in her category fairly easily. That in itself made the decision to go ahead and audition worthwhile. She was now a *Star Search* winner. She was also $3,500 richer, and for Rosie in those years that was a lot richer.

But she wasn't spending the money in Hollywood. She lived as cheaply as possible—a minor hotel near the studio, hot dog dinners—aiming to save as much as possible for the future. Rosie was the first female winner among the comics, and she went on winning for another four weeks. That meant that she was eligible for the semifinals, to be held later in the year. In the interim she went back to Long Island. There she found herself being recognized on the street and at the mall by people who had never been to a comedy club but had seen her on *Star Search*. Rosie the fan, who had always been elated to spot a star, even at a distance, was finally getting a small taste of what it might feel like to be one herself.

However, when she returned to Hollywood for the semifinals, Rosie met with disappointment. This kind of competition is tough in any category because the closer a competitor gets to the big prize, the more of his or her regular material gets used up. It's easier for singers, since there are thousands of famous songs they can draw on in preparing new material. A stand-up comic has to create new material out of whole cloth. Even with the break before the semifinals, Rosie's repertoire of jokes was getting a little thin. She was beaten by a slightly more experienced comic, John Kassir, who went on to a good if not spectacular career. Being a semifinal loser added only another $1,500 to her winnings, but they still added up to nearly $20,000, which she has called "a huge amount of money" at the time.

With this nest egg, she decided to stay in Hollywood, her head filled with dreams of being cast by Steven Spielberg or some other star director. Unfortunately, Hollywood didn't regard *Star Search* as such a big deal. She wasn't even able to get a booking at the famous Hollywood Improv comedy club. You needed to have a considerable background as a headliner at smaller clubs to be taken seriously at the Improv. The best that could be said about her Hollywood stay was that for the first time a star actually recognized her. This was more exciting than having people stop her at a mall on Long Island. Robin Williams, who had graduated from TV's *Mork and Mindy* to star in such movies as *Popeye* (1980) and *The World According to Garp* (1982), and was currently starring in *Moscow on the Hudson,* often showed up at the Improv to try out new material. He saw Rosie there, recognized her from *Star Search,* and greeted her. "I was like, 'Oh, my God, Robin Williams said hello to me,' " Rosie would later recall.

But her *Star Search* appearances did count with other clubs around the country, and she began to line up some dates where she was made the headliner, which meant that she went on last. That can be a mixed blessing, similar to getting the final curtain call in a stage production of any kind. If the audience responds more warmly to someone else, taking that star bow, or topping off the evening at a club, can be an embarrassing experience. It was one that Rosie went through on her very first gig as a headliner. She was appearing at the Comedy Castle in Detroit. There were two other comics on the bill, and the one who went on just before her was a hometown boy who knew just how to get through to their audiences. What's more, he was very funny—one of the few comics on the circuit at that time who would make it very big, just as Rosie would. His name was Tim Allen. Rosie was fortunate because Allen has a reputation for niceness right up there with her own, and he proved it by agreeing to her request that he take over the final spot from her. She didn't offer to make up the difference in their salaries—a headliner always makes more—because she thought that having the opportunity to cap off the evening was enough. A dozen years later, when he was a guest on her talk show, and she thanked him sincerely for what he had done in Detroit, and for not even bringing up the money question at the time, Tim Allen was able to get a big laugh from the studio audience—and from Rosie herself—by saying, "But you still owe me eleven hundred dollars."

• • •

In 1984, when I was a stand-up comic, I called [Bette Midler's] fan club and got her De-Tour concert schedule. I booked myself in the same cities where she was appearing, and then I called in sick at comedy clubs so I could go see her. I saw her 26 times.

So given all this obsession, you can imagine how terrified I was the first time Bette and I met. It was several years ago—I was going to the wedding of one of her Harlette backup singers with a friend who was also a friend of Bette's. The three of us rode in the same limo to the wedding. I felt absolutely sick to my stomach. There she was! The Queen of All Things! Her Highness! My idol! Bette now says this was the longest limo ride of her life because I just wouldn't shut up, or stop singing. It was her biggest nightmare: being trapped with the fan from hell.

Rosie O'Donnell in *McCall's*, May 1997

• • •

In fact, though Rosie probably didn't realize it at the time, it was entirely possible that Tim Allen was actually making more money doing the second spot than she was getting as the headliner. The comedy clubs had never heard of "equal pay for equal work." Women got less than men, sometimes even if they were supposedly bigger names. It was some time before Rosie figured this out. At one club she developed a friendly relationship with the woman who kept the books for the club. As Rosie recalls, the woman said, " 'There must be a mistake here. It says you're only getting seven hundred dollars to headline. It must be seventeen hundred, right?' I was getting less than half of what the men would get."

Even so, she was making a decent living now, with regular engagements. And over the next two years she was able to get jobs as the opener for a number of star acts. That was exciting to Rosie the fan, and important to Rosie the performer. Some performers, whether singers, music groups, or comics, never get beyond being an opener. It is still a big step up from the comedy clubs. The halls are much bigger, giving the performer a chance to learn how to handle a larger crowd, and being an opener gives someone on his or her way up steadily growing credibility. Rosie opened for some important acts: The Temptations in Atlantic City, David Copperfield in Las Vegas, and, most exciting for her, Dolly Parton on a considerable tour. As might be expected, the two down-home, unpretentious women hit it off very well. Dolly Parton once said of herself, "It takes a lot of money to look this trashy." That's right in tune with Rosie making fun of her own weight problem.

In between these stints as an opening act, Rosie was now

able to get more frequent bookings at the better-known comedy clubs. One of these was Iggy's Comedy Cabaret in West Hollywood. Appearing on the same bill was Dana Carvey, whom she'd worked with before. At thirty-one, Carvey was an old hand on the comedy circuit and had also appeared on a couple of short-lived television series. One night in mid-1986, there was a rumor at Iggy's that there would be some entertainment bigwigs in the audience. Such bigwigs often turn out to be someone's uncle Arnie whose brother-in-law runs the supply room at an agency. In this case, two very important people did show up: Brandon Tartikoff, the head of NBC programming, and Lorne Michaels, the executive producer of *Saturday Night Live.* They were there to take a hard look at Carvey, who was being considered a strong prospect for Michaels's show, always in need of new blood.

There are several variations on what happened next, some suggesting that Tartikoff caught Rosie's act by chance, others that he was begged by someone in Rosie's camp to stay and watch her. At any rate, he did see her. Tartikoff was famous for having the needs of every NBC show in his head at all times, making it possible for him to react to the unexpected with surprising speed. One show that was on his mind was the Nell Carter sitcom *Gimme a Break,* which had been on for five seasons as a middling success. Carter's chief foil on the series, character actor Dolph Sweet, had died of cancer in May 1985, and the 1985–1986 season had not been able to compensate properly for his loss. Still, Tartikoff had decided to try to fix it, and was looking for ways to give it a shot of adrenaline.

Rosie O'Donnell certainly had the sharp presence that makes people sit up and take notice, and Tartikoff immediately thought of his *Gimme a Break* problem. Maybe she was the answer. The show's producers and writers were enthusiastic about the idea, too, but even so, Rosie wasn't immediately given a season contract. Instead, she was thrust into a trial-by-fire situation. She would guest star on one of the first fall episodes, and if viewers liked her, she would be made a permanent part of the cast. This was not an unusual approach to take with an established show. Sometimes it worked, sometimes it didn't. What it did do was put the performer involved on the spot. Rosie had met other such challenges, as when the club owner told her if she didn't go over he wouldn't hire any more female comics, and her first *Star Search* appearance. She met this one, too.

From childhood Rosie had wanted to be an actress. Stand-up comedy had just been a route to that goal, and even as she had risen through the ranks of comedians to become a headliner, she had continued to want to go beyond that. Now she felt she would have that opportunity. But *Gimme a Break* didn't prove to be the breakthrough she hoped it would be.

THREE

Getting Places

The most strained atmosphere in show business probably is that of a Broadway-bound play or musical that is bombing in tryouts on the road (or nowadays for musicals, right on Broadway, which is even worse). The next most difficult situation may be that of a sitcom on its last legs. *Gimme a Break* had never been a Top Twenty television hit, but it had drawn a big enough audience to keep going through five seasons, surviving even the death of one of its two central performers. The show had been conceived around Nell Carter, who had won a Tony for a show-stopping performance in the musical revue *Ain't Misbehavin'* on Broadway. Her personality, very brassy but with a big wink, had seemed ideal for a sitcom.

However, by the sixth season, when Rosie joined the cast, it was clear that Nell Carter was running out of steam. The background for the show was shifted from a California town to New York City, where Nell now had a job in publishing and her great good friend Addy, played by Telma Hopkins, taught at an area college. The household also included Grandpa Kanisky (the father of Dolph Sweet's original police chief) and two orphan boys, one of whom, played by the young Joey Lawrence, was already a regular, while the other, played by Joey's real-life younger brother Matthew, was a newcomer. Also new to the New York setting were Paul Sand as the addled landlord of their apartment building, and Rosie as (what else?) an upstairs neighbor—a dental technician from Boston named Maggie O'Brien. The role allowed her to make use of the Irish accent she had long employed in her stand-up routines about her father. Maggie was, of course, full of wisecracks.

All of this was fairly derivative. Rosie herself described her character as "Rhoda Morgenstern with an Irish accent." This was fine by Rosie—it allowed her to send a note to her Boston University drama teacher who had told her that the part of Rhoda had already been cast, and that she'd never get anywhere, giving him what for. By the time the first episode of the new season was taped, the producers had decided that Maggie was a useful foil and plot enhancer, and Rosie was given a full year's contract.

It was not an entirely happy experience. It's always difficult for a new cast member to fit into the offstage dynamics of a group that's been working together for some time, and matters were not helped by the fact that Nell Carter was unhappy with the whole situation. Possibly she was just burned out (something that happens to the stars of most sitcoms), but it has also been suggested that she became even more unhappy when she discovered that Rosie was getting many of the best laughs. Rosie knew better than to bad-mouth Carter at the time, but in 1988, after the show was off the air, she did tell David Friedman of *Newsday*, the Long Island newspaper, "Nell always called me Maggie and I don't think it's because she's into the Stanislavsky method." In fact, it is a well-worn prima donna ploy in the theater, movies, and television to call an actress or actor by their character's name even off-camera, as though to suggest that the star can't quite recall the performer's real name. By the time Rosie became a full-fledged star herself, though, Nell Carter appeared on her talk show and suggested that Rosie had been one of the people on *Gimme a Break* she had *not* been unhappy with. Rosie let it pass.

Rosie had long dreamed of being on a sitcom. Not only did the reality of achieving her dream fail to measure up as a career breakthrough (the show was canceled at the end of the season), but it had been a less than pleasant experience even while the show was in production. It left a sour taste in her mouth. "I thought I've climbed this mountain and there's nothing there," she would later tell *US* magazine.

Yet it had been a more important experience than Rosie realized at the time. It *was* an acting job, and she'd done it well. Although we all know about the stars who have moved from stand-up to acting and been great successes—people like Tim Allen and Ellen DeGeneres—there are many who show up briefly in a sitcom and then disappear from sight. Rosie may have feared she, too, might sink into oblivion, but in fact nobody blamed her for the decline of *Gimme a Break*. It had been on its last legs, anyway. Having been in the show gave Rosie a new kind of credibility; casting agents instead of just club owners now had her in the backs of their minds. And in terms of exposure, she'd been seen by a whole new audience. What's more, she'd learned a lot. The technical aspects of appearing on a sitcom are very different than simply moving to center stage on a show like *Star Search*. You have to move around a set, make snappy entrances and exits, play to the camera in a different way, and interact with a group of actors. It's good training. In one sense, Rosie now had completed the kind of course in acting she never got a chance to take in college or at a drama school, and she passed with ease as several million viewers watched.

But for months after the last taping of *Gimme a Break,* Rosie felt low. It was necessary to go back on the road as a stand-up comic, and that was something she had thought she would be moving beyond. But her spirits were actually restored by this return to her roots. All the clubs were happy to have her, she was getting more money, and audiences were responding to her as a somebody instead of as a wannabe. One of the clubs she had been unable to get a gig at two years ago was the L.A. Improv. Not only was she now a welcome performer there, but the owner, Budd Friedman, steered her toward her next step forward. Friedman, who had liked Rosie even before he thought she was quite ready for his important club, had as much knowledge about what was going on in the business as anybody around. His own show, *An Evening at the Improv,* had been appearing on the

Arts & Entertainment cable channel for two years, and he had his ear to the ground when it came to television in general. He had heard that MTV was interested in finding a female "veejay" to give hip, funny commentary between music videos. Some women comics were leery of this type of job, feeling that it wouldn't work with the personas they had developed or wouldn't really give them a chance to shine. There was in fact a "traffic cop" aspect to hosting—the viewers were primarily tuned in for the videos, after all—but Rosie saw that the situation could offer some real benefits for her. "I needed a change," she said, "a new challenge. I saw it as an opportunity to let a lot of people know me and be distinguished from the many female comics who were working the circuit."

But MTV producers didn't think she was right for that particular slot. They didn't tell her why, but she herself came to the conclusion that, "I wasn't hip enough, the traditional thin, young, heavy-rocker." The MTV people obviously saw something they liked because they let her know that there was an opening on VH-1 that she might be right for instead. VH-1 (standing for Video Hits One) had been on the air since 1985, showing videos by pop stars like Barry Manilow. The channel was now moving toward presenting more rock videos, but had to be careful not to include too much of the more cutting-edge material that appeared on MTV. MTV and VH-1 were sister channels, under combined ownership, and it was necessary to keep them from competing too directly with one another. As part of the changeover to a somewhat hipper format, VH-1 wanted its own group of veejays.

And if Rosie wasn't quite hip enough for MTV, she proved to be just what VH-1 was looking for.

By accepting this job, Rosie was in a way settling for second best. VH-1 was a channel, in fact, that some of her fellow comedians made fun of, and there were certainly those who thought she was foolish to sign up with it. It did reach twenty-eight million homes. And Rosie had never seen herself as a cutting-edge type, anyway—her gift was for making everyday life funny. On top of that, Rosie was tired of the road, and by settling into a New York job, she would be able to see more of her family. She missed her brothers and particularly her sister Maureen, who now had a young daughter.

• • •

I meet a lot of celebrities in my life—Darren from Be-
witched—I saw him in Ralph's Supermarket. I'm not sure if
he was the first or second Darren. Remember that? When
you were a kid, they just switched Darrens and never ex-
plained why. I would always be looking at my father—
"Daddy? Just checking." See, it was scary.

Rosie O'Donnell on *Stand-up Spotlight,* 1988

• • •

She began in April 1988. "VH-1 is perfect for me right now," she said. "I get to talk about my life, my weight,

Whitney Houston's ego problems, whatever pops into my head. It certainly beats working for a living." In fact, she was working extremely hard. Twenty-four three-minute Rosie segments were broadcast each day, and although they were taped in advance and inserted where applicable, with some being repeated, the schedule could sometimes be exhausting.

The producers wanted Rosie to introduce herself at the start of each segment. Rosie thought that was silly. So, early viewers of her segments were treated to her introducing herself facetiously as various singers of the moment. While she was careful to choose performers whom she very obviously was not, like Chaka Khan, she soon discovered that not everybody can take a joke—especially managers. One day she introduced herself as the singer and star of Rosie's beloved old sitcom *The Brady Bunch*. This was a red flag to Florence Henderson's manager, who accused Rosie of suggesting that Henderson endorsed or was going to appear on her show. (It was not Henderson's own idea to complain, and later she would appear several times on Rosie's talk show.) But it put an end to such hijinks for the moment.

Rosie got a few jokes played on her, too. Long before her famous Tom Cruise crush, Rosie fixated humorously on the Olympic diver Greg Louganis, who in the summer of 1988 was repeating his 1984 triumph in Los Angeles by winning two Gold Medals at Seoul, South Korea. When Louganis returned to the United States and heard about Rosie's fantasy of encountering him in his swimsuit, he dropped in on her during a taping, wearing nothing but his Speedo. The cameraman knew what was up, and swiveled the camera to take in the action as she charged Louganis—after first letting out an astonished scream.

Louganis stayed and talked with her. This was one of the many aspects of the VH-1 job that helped give her the experience to launch her own major talk show eight years later. She was also learning how to time segments, how to use anything that was going on in the world around her to enliven those segments, and getting used to the special scrutiny of the camera in a "talking head" format—something quite different from the environment of a sitcom like *Gimme a Break*. The one thing that really gave her pause was working without an audience. "I never know if I'm going over."

During this period, she also made headlining appearances at the famous clubs Catch a Rising Star and Chicago Improv, getting some nice reviews at both. These reviews took special notice of what Bill Ervolino of the *New York Post* dubbed "a master's degree in pop culture." Critics can be dumb sometimes, but in Rosie's case it was noted early on that she had a real gift for plugging into the television and music trivia that elicited a knowing chuckle from audiences.

While her segments were clearly a success, VH-1 was still trying to figure out how to expand its audience and develop a clearer identity. The decisions that were made suddenly cast Rosie back into limbo. There were not going to be any more veejay segments. Instead, the channel decided to go with half-hour specials with particular music artists. Rosie's contract was still in effect as the changeover was made in 1989, and VH-1 told her they would buy it out.

Rosie could have decided on a "take the money and run" course of action. Instead, she made them an offer they couldn't refuse. She suggested that she host a half-hour program (which would fit in with the new format), on which she would act as host, do a brief stand-up routine, and then introduce two established comics and one newcomer. Not only was this a smart idea that Rosie was clearly capable of making work, but she made it hard to refuse by asking for no additional pay unless the show went past twenty episodes. This meant that instead of paying Rosie just to unload her contract, VH-1 would get some actual "product" out of the deal. There was a good deal of back-and-forth bargaining; the upshot was that Rosie would also be the executive producer of the show, but would have to put together her own pilots. To pull that off, Rosie drew on a lot of connections she had established over the years, even getting a TV production crew to work for free with the promise that they'd be used if the show was accepted.

It was. The first thirteen episodes were taped at a West Orange, New Jersey, club called Rascals (where the pilots had also been made), but then the venue was moved to Pasadena, California, and to the stage of the Ice House, a club whose two hundred seats were ranged in a wide half-circle that kept the audience very close and that was also perfect for filming.

The show was called *Stand-up Spotlight,* and although as

host Rosie had that spotlight trained on her during every episode, she also used it to showcase the talents of numerous comics she had worked with over the years, including Vinnie Mark, with whom she had shared the bill at the very start of her career at the Eastside Comedy Club on Long Island. When comics appeared on television, it was usually in a show that used many more musical acts than comedians, and they tended to feel a little like interlopers. This situation was changing by the late 1980s as more and more comedy specials were being broadcast, but numerous comics were nevertheless thrilled by the treatment they received when they showed up to do *Stand-up Spotlight*. With no musical guests, and a fellow comic as executive producer, they were made to feel terrifically welcome. Rosie's warmth and respect for their talents made them feel like kings and queens for a day. She even gave everyone who appeared on the show gifts of a robe and a travel bag with the VH-1 logo on them. The gift giving that is today such a charming aspect of *The Rosie O'Donnell Show* goes way back.

The fledgling comedians, of which there was one each show, got the same treatment as the established stars of the comedy circuit. Rosie didn't have to search very hard for newcomers; as soon as the show began appearing, the audition tapes began pouring in. For the first time, Rosie O'Donnell was not just one comic looking for advancement on the circuit, but was in a position to help shape the future of American stand-up comedy.

Being a good comic is one thing. Being in charge of a television show is quite another, and many good comics can't do that organizational job. But Rosie had long ago learned to be efficient. Not only had she helped run the O'Donnell household after her mother's death, but just keeping her ever-growing collection of show business memorabilia in order had taught her organizational skills from an early age. Although she already had the cast of mind that makes a good executive producer, she learned an enormous amount while hosting and producing *Stand-up Spotlight*. To produce and perform simultaneously requires a unique ability to sell yourself to an audience even as you keep a "third eye" on production concerns. Even those who have the aptitude for it need a lot of practice to become completely at ease with sometimes conflicting priorities, and Rosie was getting it in a big way. She was laying the groundwork for coping with the demands of a daily show in the yet unforeseen future.

In her opening slot on the show, Rosie needed a lot of new material on a regular basis. For any comic, there are tried-and-true subjects that can be set up in a way that makes them their own. Here's Rosie dealing with golf on *Stand-up Spotlight*:

"Really, golf is not a sport. Golf is men in ugly pants walking. I watched this game, I figured it out. Oh, don't boo that. It's so boring. They put it on television. And it's so dull. Just to make the game a little more dull, for the viewing audience at home, the announcers whisper so they don't wake up the people sleeping in front of their television sets. . . . I'm thinking of going into golf announcing myself. No, really, I am. I've been practicing. [*Whispering*] 'Hi,

Rosie O'Donnell here, yeah, okay, Arnold Palmer's about to [*screaming*]: PUTT, PUTT, PUTT.' "

As time went on, Rosie took the step that any comedian with a regular show eventually must: She hired writers to develop some of her material. When a comic reaches that point, it's clear that success has arrived. The demand for "product" has begun to exceed the capacity of a single person to provide it. The writers must be in sync with the particular comic, and eventually they begin to run out of material that suits that person, too. The reason why every television show hires and fires writers at a fast clip doesn't necessarily have anything to do with the star being difficult; rather, it's the fact that television devours new material faster than any other medium of entertainment in show business history. In the days of vaudeville, comics could get through a whole year with a single set of jokes because they were always being delivered to a new audience in a new town or city. The best of them always tried to add a topical joke based on current news, but basically they could use the same material for a very long time. Television put an end to that.

Television wasn't the only entertainment industry that devoured material. Hollywood was having so much trouble finding new scripts that could pass muster with studio executives devoted to the "high concept" mode of movie making that it started digging up old television shows from which to make movies. "High concept" means that the idea for the movie can be explained to a seventh-grader in two sentences. Hollywood had many fine, sophisticated scripts that had been floating around for years, but they often required an entire page to explain, and studio executives, with their certainty that the American public was terminally dumb, didn't want anything that complicated. Why not make movies out of old television series that the public was already familiar with?

Later on, some of these movies would be hits, like 1994's *Maverick*, and 1995's *The Brady Bunch*. Others, like *The Coneheads* and *Dennis the Menace*, would not. (The *Star Trek* movies were all hits, of varying degrees, but they were in a class by themselves.) Rosie would herself end up in one of the bigger successes, 1994's *The Flintstones*, but the first recycled TV property she was involved with was destined for disaster. *Car 54, Where Are You?* was based on a short-lived 1961–1963 series on NBC. This slapstick police-precinct sitcom hadn't exactly burned up the airwaves in the first place. Why make a movie of it?

The answer was the success of the equally silly series of *Police Academy* movies. Critical response to these movies is best summed up by quoting Mick Martin and Marsha Porter's *Video Movie Guide:* "It's like a curse. Each spring a new *Police Academy* film is released. And each year, for several weeks, it becomes the number-one movie in America." This was their reaction to number 4 in the series, released in 1987. Two more would follow, and whatever critics thought of them, teenaged males flocked to them.

So *Car 54, Where Are You?* seemed like a good enough potential moneymaker for Orion Pictures to agree to distribute it. Orion was an independent company that usually distributed films of a fairly high-class nature. But Orion was already in financial trouble, even though word hadn't really gotten out on how much trouble, and it needed something to bring in some bucks. To take the parts originated on television by Joe E. Ross and Fred Gwynne, producer Bill Fishman cast David Johanson, best known in his singing persona as Buster Poindexter, and John C. McGinley, who had been in the Oliver Stone movies *Platoon* (1986) and *Talk Radio* (1989). In *Car 54* Johanson played the utterly goofy Gunther Toody and McGinley the not much brighter but dour Francis Muldoon. Rosie was asked to read for the role of Toody's wife, Lucille, and was eventually hired despite some resistance from Orion.

In the movies at last! Rosie was thrilled, but soon discovered a fact that even Elizabeth Taylor has bemoaned about movie making—as Rosie would put it, she thought she was ". . . gonna be working, working, working. Most of it was waiting, waiting, waiting, you know." She got little directorial help on the two-month shoot in Toronto, Canada, which went on from the end of August to the end of October 1990. Even before the movie wrapped, word was out that Orion was in really deep trouble financially. It soon declared bankruptcy. That put *Car 54* into limbo for more than three years. Another Orion film that spent more than three years on the shelf was *Blue Sky*, but although it was a commercial flop, Jessica Lange's heartbreaking performance as a mentally unstable army wife brought her the Oscar as Best Actress for 1994. Rosie wasn't anywhere near that fortunate.

When *Car 54* was finally released in 1994, it met with a

hostility that critics reserve for really bad movies on days when they're in a really bad mood. Everyone in the movie was panned, and Rosie came in for her share of nasty comments, which drew upon such evocative phrases as "flailing around," "one-note hollering," "nearly unwatchable." The best that could be said was that a number of critics suggested that she and several of the other cast members should be looked upon as "wasted talent."

In the end, Rosie had been lucky the movie was shelved for so long. She still had her VH-1 show, and since no one knew how bad *Car 54* actually was, a movie that could have ended her film career on the spot if it had been released on schedule was simply a line on her résumé that showed she had had movie experience. It was her VH-1 work that would bring her a major breakthrough in a movie half the women in Hollywood wanted to be in.

FOUR

A Different League

When the new movie directed by Penny Marshall, called *A League of Their Own*, opened in July 1992, nobody did more publicity interviews for it than Rosie O'Donnell. She had fifth billing, after Tom Hanks, Geena Davis, Lori Petty, and Madonna, but no one was more fun to interview about the film, and no one was more enthusiastic about it. Rosie told one interviewer after another, "When I read the script, I thought, 'My God, if I don't get this movie, I should quit show business.'"

She had good reason to feel that way. The movie was a comedy, and Rosie was by now a nationally known funny lady. But that was only part of it. *A League of Their Own* was about a women's baseball team, inspired by an actual women's league that existed during and for a short while after World War II. When she was interviewed by former major league catcher Joe Garagiola on *Today*, Rosie explained that when she was a kid, girls weren't allowed to play in Little League, but her two older brothers were on the local team on Long Island. ". . . So I would go down with them while they were working out . . . and the coach would let me play because he thought it was so funny that this little eight-year-old girl could catch fly balls in the outfield. So I would play before the game and after the game and put on my brother's uniform when he was at school and pretend like I was in Little League." In another interview, she recalled, "I was always the first girl picked for the neighborhood teams. I got picked ahead of my three brothers, which I think still affects them."

Since the cast of *A League of Their Own* was mostly women, word about the script had traveled like wildfire around Hollywood and New York. While a great many actresses wanted to have a part in the movie, Rosie figured that "if there's one thing I can do better than Meryl Streep and Glenn Close, it's play baseball." In fact, baseball came first in terms of importance in the auditioning. Rosie flew out to Los Angeles, where actresses were required to show off their baseball skills at the diamond on the University of Southern California campus. "It was really funny," Rosie recounted later. "They had about two hundred women about ten times in a row go down to U.S.C. and audition with each other. And they filmed us on video, hitting and running and throwing and catching. And it was really funny to see all these actresses who had never played baseball who had lied to their agents and said, 'Oh, yeah, I can play.' Like, you know, these really thin Barbie doll–like women.

And I'm like, 'Honey, hold the thin end of the bat, OK? Good luck out there. Be careful out there.' "

Rosie passed the baseball audition with flying colors. It was decided that her character, Doris, should play third base because she was one of the few women who could throw from third to first consistently, and "without a lot of ice on my shoulder" after a day's shooting. The character itself was also rewritten and enlarged for Rosie. "The part was originally for a hot, sexy girl," director Penny Marshall admitted, "but I liked Rosie so much we changed the story to suit her. She can make anything funny." Marshall had seen some of Rosie's shows, and seen to it that she was sent a script. In the film Rosie was supposed to be the best friend of another player on the team who hadn't yet been cast. Penny Marshall wanted Madonna for that role, and Rosie remembers Marshall saying, "If she likes me and she likes you, she'll do the movie. Be funny."

Madonna did do the movie, reportedly causing Debra Winger, who was set to play the lead role of the team catcher and leader, to drop out. Geena Davis, who was brought in as a replacement, had a lot of catching up to do on the field. Davis later said, "It was daunting, but I think I thrive on challenge, or seemingly impossible tasks." But if Davis was daunted by the work ahead of her, Rosie was intimidated by another aspect of the job. Geena Davis was an established star and had already won an Academy Award as Best Supporting Actress for 1988's *The Accidental Tourist*. Rosie was a neophyte, with only a small part in a movie that might never be released to her credit. "It was such a powerhouse cast, Madonna and Tom Hanks, Geena Davis, Penny Marshall. You know, Penny, Geena, and Madonna are three of the most powerful women in Hollywood. So it was very intimidating initially. I felt like a dork, you know, meeting Madonna."

. . .

Rosie on Madonna: "She's some exotic food, and I'm just a peanut-butter-and-jelly sandwich."

Madonna on Rosie: "We both have a longing for strong female role models. We like to be the center of attention and make people laugh. We both like to sing, though obviously my voice is more mainstream than hers. Our personal lives are a mess. And we both love candy."

To Patrick Pacheo, in *Cosmopolitan,* June 1994

. . .

"What do you say to Madonna?" Rosie recalled asking herself. "How do you bond with Madonna? What do you say? 'Hi, I have a vibrator'? What do you say to her? She is so wild, I didn't know what to do." However, Rosie had seen Madonna's revelatory documentary *Truth or Dare* twice, and had noticed similarities in their lives. "My mom died when I was a little girl, as did hers, and I'm named after my mom, as is she. And we both come from large

Catholic families. So when I saw the film, I was really touched by how many similarities there are in our lives. And I thought if I ever met her I would have a lot to say to her." Rosie says that she stammered around a lot at the beginning, when she did meet Madonna, but then calmed down and remembered to talk about the things they shared in their pasts. "I think I told her in the first ten minutes that my mother died when I was a young kid, as did hers, and so that created this sort of sisterly-like relationship that has continued since we met," Rosie later told Joe Garagiola.

When he heard this, Garagiola mentioned that he had been intimidated when he first met the legendary Red Sox left fielder Ted Williams at the 1946 World Series. Rosie, demonstrating command of a whole new realm of trivia, responded, "Well, you know, Joe, in 1946 you were twenty years old. You had four hits in that World Series." Garagiola was suitably impressed, but it seems likely that Rosie had simply done her homework before talking to Garagiola, since she would admit in another interview that she didn't quite get some aspects of baseball fandom. Much of the filming for *A League of Their Own* was done at the home of the Chicago Cubs, storied Wrigley Field. Rosie told *Premiere* magazine that fellow actress Robin Knight "was picking up little pieces of dirt off the mound and putting them in Ziploc bags to take home. I thought she was on crack. I'm thinking, 'What the hell are you doing?' She's like, 'It's Wrigley Field, man!' I guess for me it would be like being in Bette Midler's dressing room."

While they were at Wrigley Field, there were often hundreds of extras sitting in the stands, who would be called on to cheer or boo in reaction to what was being filmed. But the cast spent a lot of time waiting around for a new shot to be set up. Even Hollywood stars often admit that this aspect of making movies can lead to a great deal of boredom. However, the stars have trailers to retire to while the extras just have to sit and wait. "It was my job sort of to entertain the audience while Penny and [the crew] got the shots ready," Rosie recounted later. "She'd come over and [*nasal voice*], 'Rosie, they're getting bored, go *do* something.' And they'd hand me the mike. So for thirty minutes I'd be singing *The Brady Bunch* theme, and do stand-up for five thousand extras. When Geena, or Tom, was not too busy, I'd go, 'Ladies and gentlemen, here's Tom Hanks.' And Tom would come out and do something. And then I'd go, 'Oh, you want to hear from Madonna, do you? *Madonna!*' Everyone participated."

Geena Davis reported that she liked to sing "Bohemian Rhapsody," even though nobody knew it because it was a very old song. But Geena knew all the words, as did Rosie. So the two of them, joined by a couple of others, "would sing this at the top of our lungs . . . but now it's like this gigantic hit, because it's in *Wayne's World*." Obviously, this was a cast having a good time. Tom Hanks said, "Look, the whole reason I did this movie was because it was going to be a blast. Come on—play baseball all summer with a bunch of girls? Please! Help me. And get paid to do it? Fine, I'm there. When do we start?" Hanks no doubt also realized that the role of the over-the-hill ex–major-leaguer hired to manage this all-girl team was a terrific part. Long recognized as one of Hollywood's most likable leading men, he had even been nominated for a Best Actor Oscar for 1988's *Big*. This role, however, was a character part, with a darker side to it, and it would cause critics to see a new dimension in his acting that would presage his later triumphs in his Oscar-winning performances in *Philadelphia* and *Forrest Gump*.

Hanks had put on weight to play this role. Rosie had been asked to take weight off. Penny Marshall wanted her to lose twenty pounds. "And I'm like, 'Oh sure, Pen. No problem,'" Rosie recalled later, adding, "If I could lose twenty pounds, I would. I wouldn't have to have Penny tell me. It's not like I don't own a mirror." When it came down to it, Rosie thought she probably gained weight while making the movie. She blamed it on the good food laid out every day for the crafts people working on the set. To audiences and critics who saw the movie, Rosie's chubbiness just made her funnier and more endearing as she hustled around the ballfield like a little dynamo.

Filming went on six days a week. It was a grueling schedule, made more intense by the enormous amount of physical work involved. There were intensive training and workout sessions before the filming even began, which everyone took very seriously. Except that Madonna managed to get into the tabloids again because of some extra help she sought. As Pepper Davis, the former women's baseball star who worked with the cast, told Nancy Griffin of *Premiere*: "Did you read in the papers about Jose Canseco? Well, he was seen goin' out to Madonna's apartment at three in the morning. He was giving her baseball tips, but nobody believed it. See, she wanted to be in the movie in the worst way. And so I guess she called up Canseco, and he came out to her apartment, and—oh, the papers made a big flap out of it." Rosie later had her own take on this story. When Joe Garagiola asked if the American League slugger was really Madonna's batting coach, Rosie replied, "I think so, honey. But I don't know what kind of bat we're talking here. Thank you and goodnight!"

In Chicago the professionals hired to coach the actresses in baseball technique decided to train them on a Slip 'N Slide used by Little Leaguers. But after Megan Cavanagh and Tracy Reiner got concussions trying that approach, it was abandoned. Even so, as filming progressed, everyone was covered with bruises, some people had to have stitches, and there was at least one broken nose. But all the coaching was paying off. "I was in batting practice,'" Rosie recalled, "and I'm hitting away, and Pepper said to me, 'Rosie.' I go, 'Yeah?' 'Move your right foot.' 'Which way?' 'Point it up, point it up.' So I move my right foot, honestly, an inch forward. Oh my God—boom! You know. And she just nodded and walked away."

When they were filming, a great many takes were made of each segment of actual baseball action. Penny Marshall was well known for liking to film many takes of even a conversational scene in a small room, but the need to get the baseball play to conform to the script meant even more grueling retakes. Later Rosie would say that Penny Marshall was the "queen of the retakes," which made her by now good friend Penny angry. "She's like, 'Rosie, I don't do retakes, I do coverage, coverage.' That's what she does. We'll shoot from this angle. We'll do it like ten times. 'OK, moving in. OK, action. OK, moving in, moving.' You know, so she shot every scene from every conceivable angle that you could do it. But actually it's very beneficial because you end up having a lot of opportunities to do the same scene over and over again and she has a lot of film to work with to edit together for a final product."

When she related this story to Mark McEwan on *CBS This Morning*, he asked if it was strange having Laverne direct her in a movie. "It was," Rosie admitted. "And I'm such a huge *Laverne and Shirley* fan I know all these little trivia facts about Laverne and Shirley, like Boo-Boo Kitty, a stuffed animal, and how she used to drink milk and Pepsi. And I would quote lines from *Laverne and Shirley* to her, which she found amusing on some level, I think."

Rosie made two good personal friends while filming *A League of Their Own*. While she has kept in touch with Tom Hanks and Geena Davis and Lori Petty and others in the cast, Penny Marshall and Madonna are the kinds of friends that can be called up anytime just to say hello. Rosie has even called Madonna from the set of her talk show; and she and Penny have made a hilarious series of ads for Kmart that play off their teasing camaraderie to great effect.

After the film wrapped, questions could be heard in Hollywood about its potential for success. Baseball movies were regarded as a chancy business. Some, like *Bull Durham* (1988), took off, but that movie, starring Kevin Costner,

Susan Sarandon, and Tim Robbins, was as much about a quirky romantic triangle as it was about baseball. Yet, 1984's *The Natural,* despite having Robert Redford and terrific reviews, had not been a real hit. What's more, *A League of Their Own* was the most expensive baseball movie ever made. Because of the difficulty of its baseball scenes, it had had a long shooting schedule and would require a very long editing process, factors which contributed to a $50 million budget. Penny Marshall had a way with quirky material. In 1988, *Big* had followed two other little-boy-as-grown-man movies that had been flops earlier in the year, and the enormous success of Marshall's movie had taken Hollywood by complete surprise. But a baseball movie about female players, set way back in World War II? Could even the Marshall touch pull that off?

The publicity barrage for the movie was extremely well handled, however, in the weeks before its July 1992 opening. The combination of Tom Hanks, Geena Davis, and Madonna fascinated the national magazines. The fact that the story had a strong feminist element in its celebration of women athletes brought it attention from other publications, helped by the fact that providing equal-opportunity sports funding for women at schools and colleges was an ongoing national issue. It also turned out that Lori Petty, Jon Lovitz, and, particularly, Rosie O'Donnell could provide extremely vivid and funny interview copy. Indeed, as the movie opened, Rosie was being interviewed everywhere. Penny Marshall had known what she was doing when she cast Rosie. She got a much funnier and more interesting character in the story than had existed in the original script, for starters. By beefing up the role and giving Rosie ad-lib opportunities, Marshall had created an opportunity to shine that Rosie had grabbed with both hands. In addition, Rosie had done more than her part in keeping the set happy, not to mention making the extras want to keep showing up for the entertainment she provided during the long waits between camera setups. And now she was proving to be an enormous asset in publicizing the movie.

The reviews provided the movie with some good advertising quotes: "A real bittersweet charm . . ." (Roger Ebert, the Chicago *Sun-Times*); "One of the year's most cheerful, most relaxed, most easily enjoyable movies . . ." (Vincent Canby, *The New York Times*); "Amiable and ingratiating . . ." (Richard Schickel, *Time*). There were some who carped that while *A League of Their Own* was fun, it hadn't risen to the level of its possibilities, that it could have been a great movie if it had not had so many stock characters and downplayed the serious issues for laughs on too many occasions. But laughs were just what the ticket-buying public wanted, and *A League of Their Own* proved to be a major hit, eventually grossing $107 million in its domestic release. It offered an alternative to the usual glut of violent summer action movies, and because it was about baseball, women were able to drag their husbands and boyfriends to it. Of course, Madonna's being in it helped in that department.

As for the critics who thought the movie hadn't gone far enough in exploring the serious, feminist issues it raised, they were proved wrong in many respects. *A League of Their*

Own went on being discussed by women, both privately and in published references, long after it had departed theaters. It became one of those touchstone movies for women, as *Thelma and Louise* had the year before, and as *The First Wives Club* would in 1996. When the video of *A League of Their Own* was released, it proved not only very strong on the rental charts, but was also bought outright in large numbers. Penny Marshall had had a definite feminist point to make with the movie, and if some critics didn't quite recognize how strongly it came across, the women who bought the video in large numbers showed that she had succeeded in making that point.

A League of Their Own did a lot of good for the people associated with it, quite aside from any financial considerations. It cemented Penny Marshall's position as one of the two top woman directors in Hollywood along with Barbra Streisand. It gave Geena Davis her second successive big hit, following right on the heels of *Thelma and Louise.* Tom Hanks's endearingly cranky character performance alerted the critics that he was capable of creating a vivid persona that was quite different from his own. Madonna had made one flop after another, but this featured role showed that she still possessed the charm and spunk that critics had originally admired in *Desperately Seeking Susan* back in 1985. However, no one benefited more than Rosie O'Donnell.

Rosie had been lucky. The dreadful *Car 54, Where Are You?* she had made in 1990 was still unreleased because of Orion studio's financial problems. Although Rosie's part in that movie was small and she herself had not been terrible, it was such a bad movie that if it had been released on schedule it might have given Penny Marshall second thoughts about hiring her. Instead of making her debut in a major flop, Rosie was being seen across the country in a huge hit. The publicity she did for *A League of Their Own* also raised her profile on national television, with appearances on major programs like *Today* and *CBS This Morning*, and her photo appeared in a wide cross-section of magazines, from *Premiere* to *People* to *Ladies' Home Journal*. Now Hollywood definitely knew who Rosie was, and she was no longer considered just a stand-up comedian or "that funny girl on VH-1." She'd shown that she could act a role, hold her own in a powerhouse ensemble, and really add something special to a movie.

Ironically, however, Rosie had already landed her second important movie role before *A League of Their Own* was even released, and once again her VH-1 stint proved to be a crucial element in getting it. It was becoming clear that her stand-up career, which she had once seen as the "only" route into the movies, had in fact been a very smart path to choose. Nora Ephron, an experienced writer of screenplays who was now producing her movies as well, was set to be her own director for the second time, on a script she had written called *Sleepless in Seattle*. Ephron had started out as a comic essayist whose first book was a collection of her work called *Crazy Salad* (1975). She had had a major bestseller with her novel *Heartburn* (1984), based on her failed marriage to famed Watergate reporter Carl Bernstein, and had gone on to write the screenplay for the 1986 movie based on that book, which starred Meryl Streep and Jack Nicholson. She had also written the screenplays for *Silkwood* (1983), which brought her an Academy Award writing nomination, and for the huge 1989 hit *When Harry Met Sally. . . .* Ephron had screenwriting in her blood. Her parents, Henry and Phoebe Ephron, had written many Broadway plays, among which was *The Desk Set,* which they had then adapted for the screen as a 1957 vehicle for Katharine Hepburn and Spencer Tracy. They had also written the screenplays for many other movies, including *Carousel* (1956). A hit Broadway play and subsequent movie starring James Stewart and Sandra Dee, *Take Her, She's Mine* (1962), had actually been based on letters that their daughter Nora had written home from college.

Keeping things in the family, Nora had written the script for *Sleepless in Seattle* with her younger sister, Delia. She had her stars, Tom Hanks and Meg Ryan, but there were a number of secondary roles for which she wanted fresh talent. Rosie got an audition with her. "I went in to read for it about a year ago, January, and *A League of Their Own* was not out yet. She didn't know who I was, didn't know I was a comedian or anything," Rosie told Charles Gibson on *Good Morning America*. This was a little surprising. The first movie Nora Ephron had directed had been *This Is My Life* (1992), a small but well-received film starring Julie Kavner, about a single mother who succeeds in carving out a career as a stand-up comic!

If Ephron didn't know who Rosie was, Rosie had a very important fan ready to play backup. As Rosie tells it, she read for Nora Ephron, "and she went home that night and said to her son, 'Jacob,' she said, 'I—this girl came in and she was kind of funny. I never heard of her, Rosie O'Donnell.' And he's like, 'Mom, she's on VH-1, she's funny, you should get her, I love her.' So that's the reason, she said, that she was swayed to hire me, was her thirteen year-old son."

Nora Ephron confirmed that although she had been taken with Rosie at her audition, she'd been worried about casting an "unknown." But when she mentioned Rosie to her kids, ". . . they looked at me like, 'You're even older and more washed up than we've dreamed.' " So Rosie got the coveted role of Meg Ryan's editor and boss at the Baltimore newspaper where they both worked. The character, Becky, was also Meg Ryan's best friend in the story, with a number of funny and important scenes as Meg Ryan's Annie Reed struggles with her feelings about Tom Hanks, the widowed Seattle father whose son gets him involved with a radio call-in show that dubs him "Sleepless in Seattle."

Rosie had been afraid that *A League of Their Own* might get her typecast in tomboy roles, but the role of Becky was something quite different. As a successful career woman, she was given a snazzy wardrobe and a softer, more sophisticated hairstyle. Since the character was meant to be a graduate of the Columbia School of Journalism, Nora Ephron was tough on Rosie about her accent, calling a halt to the filming if Rosie left out her "r" sounds or started to sound too streetwise. Rosie has admitted subsequently that she had needed Ephron's pickiness on such points, "because I notice in my stand-up act or when I do *Arsenio,* my accent is much thicker. It's not on purpose, it's out of nerves. When I get nervous and push it, it becomes much more streety, much more Fonzie and Sylvester Stallone-ish. She wouldn't let that happen, for which I'm glad."

Being directed by Nora Ephron also required another adjustment. Penny Marshall had not only tolerated but encouraged improvisation and ad-libs, which Rosie, with her stand-up background, was very good at. But Ephron was directing her own final script, written with David S. Ward and Jeff Arch on a story by Arch, and she wanted every word to be just as it appeared in the script. This led to Rosie sometimes hiding bits of paper with her lines on it around the set, mostly for reassurance.

She was prepared to make such adjustments. If *A League of Their Own* had allowed her to take a more improvisational approach to her role, it had nevertheless gotten her past the difficulties that many performers encounter when moving from live performance to acting on film. Even seasoned stage actors sometimes have problems in adjusting to the lack of audience response on a movie set. They are used to gauging the pace of a performance and the timing of individual lines according to the feel they get from an audience. Those working on a movie set, including all the technical personnel, have trained themselves *not* to respond—the slightest chuckle can mean another take. For stand-up comics in particular, this silence can be extremely unsettling, causing the performer to wonder instinctively what she or he is doing wrong. When *Sleepless in Seattle* was released, Rosie reminisced to Larry King about her *A League of Their*

Own experience, saying that "I'd do a joke, and I'd look around. She'd go [*imitates Penny Marshall*], 'Cut. What are you looking for?' I'd go, 'Nobody's laughing.' She's like [*imitates Penny Marshall*], 'It's a movie! They're not supposed to laugh!' So that was tough. . . ."

• • •

She is completely up-front. If she thinks something is baloney, she will say so, and she is genuinely interested in other people. She's not one of those celebrities who just wants to hear herself talk.

Nora Ephron, on Rosie, in *TV Guide*, June 15, 1996

• • •

Rosie went on to say that movies compensated for the lack of laughter on the set in many other ways, that the ensemble atmosphere of movie making took away a lot of pressure that the stand-up comic usually felt because he or she was "the writer, the editor, the director, the performer." In the movies, on the other hand, ". . . you're able to say somebody else's words in a way that someone else tells you to say it in clothing that someone else chooses. . . . It's a lot of pressure removed."

Sleepless in Seattle also presented Rosie with some real acting challenges, particularly in the scene during which Becky and Annie have to sob with emotion while watching the old Deborah Kerr/Cary Grant weeper *An Affair to Remember,* whose Empire State Building meeting between Grant and Kerr is aborted when the latter is run over by a taxi. A twist on this element was crucial to the plot of Ephron's movie. The trouble was that neither Rosie nor Meg Ryan were moved by *An Affair to Remember* in the way that their characters were supposed to be. In fact, they were moved to hysterical laughter by what they found a sappy and unbelievable story, as both women would subsequently admit. Rosie and Ryan had bonded on the set in much the same way that Rosie had bonded with Madonna on *A League of Their Own,* with movie "best friends" becoming close in real life. Their shared laughter about *An Affair to Remember* had entered into that, but it meant that they really did have to *act* their character's emotional response to the 1956 movie they were supposed to adore. Rosie was proud of being able to pull it off.

Sleepless in Seattle was the second movie in a row Rosie had made that starred Tom Hanks, but it could hardly be said that she made this one *with* Hanks, since they had no scenes together—the whole movie revolved around keeping Ryan and Hanks apart until the very end. Ironically, Hanks's wife, Rita Wilson, had wanted Rosie's part, but Rosie had already been cast before she and Hanks saw the script, when he suddenly became available because of the delay of another project. Wilson was compensated with the juicy cameo of a friend of Hanks who explains, to the

wonderment of Hanks and Rob Reiner, why women loved
An Affair to Remember.

Sleepless in Seattle was another major step forward in Rosie's movie career. It demonstrated that she had the talent
and range to play an entirely different kind of character, and
proved that she could deliver under a very different kind of
director. That in itself meant that in future she would be
thought of as an actress for a variety of projects. It was true
that in both *A League of Their Own* and *Sleepless* she was
playing a "best friend" role. But that was fine by Rosie. She
specifically brought up the career of Eve Arden. Eve had
played dozens of "best friend" parts with a freshness and
variety that made her right at home in many frothy come-
dies and musicals, but also brought her crucial roles in serious dramas like *Mildred Pierce* (1945), for which she
received a Best Supporting Actress nomination, and 1959's
sensational courtroom drama, *Anatomy of a Murder.* In addition, Eve had had a stellar radio and television career as *Our
Miss Brooks.* There was obviously nothing wrong in being
that kind of actress.

Rosie had learned a good deal while making *Sleepless in
Seattle,* which in itself made the experience a good one, but
the film also became an even bigger box office success than
A League of Their Own, taking in $126 million at the box
office. Critics were divided on the qualities of the movie,
with as many finding it contrived as charming, but audiences loved it and it became the hit comedy of the summer
of 1994. Rosie herself got numerous accolades, winning over

several critics who didn't like the movie as a whole. She was dubbed "charming," "a joy," "terrific," and "very funny," with several noting that she had many of the best lines and made the most of them.

Once again Rosie did numerous television and newspaper interviews. With two hits in two summers, when she was asked about both movies, Rosie demonstrated the humor and aplomb that had made her so popular as an interview subject. Take, for example, this exchange with Charles Gibson of *Good Morning America:*

GIBSON: You mentioned *League of Their Own* that you played in. The Mets need a third baseman. Could you be coming to New York, perhaps, to play a little third base for the Mets?

O'DONNELL: I actually am available.

GIBSON: Are you?

O'DONNELL : And I heard they made a call. I'm not saying anything, I don't want the press to get ahold of this and jump right on the story. But there's a chance. That's all I want to say about it.

GIBSON: Because you're playing better third base in that movie than some of the people that played this year.

O'DONNELL: Well, we had things called editing, which they don't really have in live baseball.

Good editing can enhance any actor's performance, of course. Rosie could also come across with great style in a live interview—something that many of Hollywood's biggest names have trouble doing. Rosie had long ago learned how to make the most of the live moment. Now she had demonstrated she could shine in movie moments, too. The ability to do both would be a key to her continuing success.

The year 1993 also saw the release of another important movie for Rosie, *Another Stakeout.* This was a sequel to 1987's *Stakeout,* starring Richard Dreyfuss and Emilio Estevez, which had been a much bigger hit than expected. The new film, produced by the Disney unit Touchstone, had the same two stars and the same director, John Badham. Although Madeleine Stowe would once again play Dreyfuss's girlfriend, the plot had an even larger role for a woman assistant district attorney named Gina Garrett, who goes along with the undercover cops, played by Dreyfuss and Estevez, on a stakeout to find a witness for an organized-crime trial, a character played by Cathy Moriarity. Rosie's role had by far the most screen time of the three main female characters. For the first time she would be playing the female lead in a movie, and it was a role that allowed her to be funny in a tart, disapproving way, but also required her to be a convincing law-enforcement figure.

She was cast after a test that showed what director Badham termed "instant sparks" with Dreyfuss. And she had a wonderful time making the movie, despite having to deal with what she would later call the "stupidest dog on the planet." Since Rosie was often attached to the other end of the dog's leash, or found herself pursuing him over hill and dale, she had plenty of opportunity to get annoyed with her canine co-star. But she adored working with both Dreyfuss and Estevez, counting their enduring friendship as one of the happiest results of making the movie.

The film is diverting, and Rosie does an excellent job of veering between seriousness and comedy. But the movie itself veered back and forth too much, according to most critics, and it was not a success at the box office. Still, it had given Rosie a starring role, showed off her range to new advantage, and had been a delight to make. Rosie could hardly complain about the way her movie career was going. No one makes only hit movies. In the past two summers, she had had important roles in the biggest comedy hit of the summer, and she was about to begin filming another movie that would extend the streak to three in a row.

FIVE

Two Bettys and a
Black Leather Corset

In 1994, Rosie O'Donnell would appear on screen in a dress made from animal hides, and in a black leather corset with garters and fishnet stockings—and she would show up on a Broadway stage in a black and pink satin warmup jacket. In the animal skins, she portrayed a Stone Age housewife, in the black leather corset she was an under-dressed undercover cop, and in the satin jacket she was the leader of a group of tough 1950s teenage girls. The first movie was *The Flintstones,* the second was *Exit to Eden,* and the Broadway show was a revival of the musical *Grease.* The critics didn't much like *The Flintstones,* hated *Exit to Eden,* and were lukewarm about *Grease.* Yet all three vehicles turned out to be good for Rosie's career, for different reasons.

The Flintstones, a TV hit during 1960–1966, was the first animated series to appear in prime time on television. It was one of the rare TV shows that Rosie felt little connection with, and had seldom watched either in reruns or its many reincarnations as specials. The original show had really been before her time; she was only three years old when it went off the air after its six-year run. But *The Flintstones* became part of American pop culture, and kept reappearing on television in one form or another at regular intervals. It just hadn't grabbed Rosie, and so she was surprised when she got a call asking if she would be interested in auditioning for the part of Betty Rubble.

The storyline for the original television series was blatantly similar to Jackie Gleason's classic *The Honeymooners*. Fred Flintstone was the same sort of blustery incompetent as Ralph Kramden, while Barney Rubble was a put-upon best friend who inevitably got dragged into Fred's trouble just as Ed Norton had on *The Honeymooners*. The two long-suffering wives were similarly required to straighten out their husbands' messes. Of course, *The Flintstones* was an animated cartoon set in the Stone Age, but the plot situations in the two shows had the same kind of structure, and the Stone Age background was supplied with anachronistic gadgets that could be played off in the same way as modern ones on *The Honeymooners*. Jackie Gleason in fact considered suing the movie studio because the shows were so much alike, but decided that it made more sense to look at the similarities as a form of flattery rather than as a ripoff.

Rosie did know enough about *The Flintstones* to realize that she was a curious possible choice for Betty Rubble: Betty was tiny, and Rosie certainly was not. But Rosie was able to do Betty Rubble's famous giggle with uncanny accuracy. And she remembered that Betty held her hands palm outward in a characteristic way. Doing her homework as always, Rosie showed up at the audition knowing the original song from the show, and lost no time in launching into it. However, it was the giggle that did it. "And I did the laugh," Rosie later recounted, ". . . and then they all started laughing. . . . And so then they thought, 'Wow, she did do that.' OK. And they hired me."

The quick decision to hire Rosie was in contrast to the history of this production, which had first been initiated in 1986. By the time the film actually began shooting in May 1993, thirty-two writers had worked on the script, an embarrassingly large number even by Hollywood standards. The production was now in the hands of Steven Spielberg and his Amblin Pictures, working with Universal Pictures. John Goodman of the TV show *Roseanne* had been cast as Fred Flintstone instead of the original choice of James Belushi. Rick Moranis had been the initial selection for Barney Rubble, then others, including Danny DeVito, had been considered, but the producers went back to Moranis in the wake of his success in *Honey, I Shrunk the Kids* and its sequel, *Honey, I Blew up the Kid*. Elizabeth Perkins landed the role of Wilma Flintstone over several other actresses, and Kyle MacLachlan of *Dune* and *Twin Peaks* was chosen to play the villain, Cliff Vandercave.

With an eye to the nostalgia game and the publicity it can generate, it was seen to that a number of well-known names were given cameo roles, including Jonathan Winters, Harvey Korman (perfect as the voice of the squawking Diktabird), Bill Hanna and Joe Barbera (co-creators of the original series), and Jean Vander Pyl, the original voice of Wilma Flintstone. Jay Leno was brought aboard as the host of "Bedrock's Most Wanted." But the real casting coup was getting Elizabeth Taylor to play Fred Flintstone's mother-in-law, Pearl Slaghoople.

Taylor hadn't made a movie in almost fifteen years, but agreed to do this role because it was small (only four days' shooting, and not all at once), funny in its shrill way, and because the producers agreed that the New York opening would be a fund-raiser for her AIDS foundation. Taylor would later say that making *The Flintstones* reminded her of why she had stopped making movies: the boredom of sitting around waiting for a scene to be shot. She also admitted that she had had fun on the set as well. Certainly everything was done to make this Hollywood legend comfortable and happy. She arrived to find the steps to her private trailer painted violet, her favorite color, and the dressing room itself was swathed in violet. Spielberg showered her with gifts at a reported cost of $10,000, including a clock from Cartier, where she had picked out many a diamond in earlier years. Taylor reciprocated this treatment, sending flowers to the set for several days before her arrival, and dispensing presents of her own.

Rosie found herself a particular recipient of Taylor's largesse. Rosie later said, "I'll tell you this, everybody was so nervous. They made all the grips—everybody—wear ties. . . . There were a zillion violets all over the place. For two hours everyone was like, 'Is she here yet? Is she here? Where is she? Is she here?' She showed up, walked in—

you know, what do you say to an Elizabeth Taylor, a living legend?" With everyone standing around more or less paralyzed, Rosie decided somebody should do something. So she went over to Taylor and said, "Hi, I have your perfume." Rosie's reward for breaking the ice was to discover a big box of Taylor's perfumes in her own trailer the next day.

In an interview just before the movie opened, Rosie said about Taylor, spoofing the instant intimacy of Hollywood, "I met her. We're very good friends." Then she added, "Actually, we did sort of become friends, which is sort of strange. But she is a lovely woman." As so often before and since, Rosie the fan was able to establish a connection with a superstar simply by being herself.

• • •

I was on a worst-dressed list, which is how I knew I was famous. Most people who don't want to be seen not looking their best go out in full makeup. But I always want to be myself. If I'm out and look like this and the paparazzi are there, I say, "Go right ahead." I don't run and hide. I'm just trying to be the same person I was in the beginning.

Rosie O'Donnell to Patrick Pacheo, in *Cosmopolitan*, June 1994

• • •

Quite aside from getting to know Elizabeth Taylor, Rosie was busy as usual trying to keep everyone happy. Reports from the set noted that she was a joy to have around, her humor helping to buoy everyone's spirits on the extremely hot outdoor location at Vasquez Rocks, forty miles northeast of Los Angeles at Agua Dulce. The location was within a county park, which meant that there were always large groups of tourists watching the filming. This created a lot of noise, and many distractions for the cast, crew, and director Brian Levant. Levant, who had directed *Beethoven,* with its canine cast, was more than up to dealing with a somewhat chaotic set, but Rosie's efforts to keep everyone smiling were appreciated. One of her ploys was to create a mock game show, focused on the career of Mary Tyler Moore— an idea she would use on her talk show in the fall of 1997. As was usual in movies she worked on, Rosie paid attention to the crew members as well as her fellow actors, an effort that is always noted in Hollywood, where prima donnas of both sexes are all too prevalent. She particularly liked to tickle John Goodman's funny bone. "He's not a guy who makes a lot of jokes himself, but when somebody makes a joke on the set he has this huge belly laugh. So I would always play to him and try to get him to crack up."

Costing $43 million to make, and with a huge promotional budget, *The Flintstones* was vulnerable to a lot of pre-release doubts on the part of the Hollywood handicappers, who enjoy nothing more than second-guessing the wisdom of making any big-budget film before its release. Between tie-ins with McDonald's restaurants and kids' vitamins in the shape of the characters—including Rosie's larger-size Betty Rubble—the public had been primed to march down to the multiplex for a cute good time. Fortunately, moviegoers were in the mood for this kind of silliness, because the critics were none too kind. Yet in a sense the naysayers allowed themselves to be co-opted by the movie in that they simply could not resist putting it down in its own terms by labeling it everything from "Yabba-Dabba-Doo-Doo" to "Yabba-Dabba-Dud." That may have led the public to suspect that the critics had had more fun than they were admitting. Or it may have been that this was one of those features where the opinion of the critics just didn't matter.

The film was released on May 17, 1994, before the real summer movie season; even so it proved to be a big hit for family viewing. It contained enough slapstick and dumb jokes to keep the kids laughing even as its more sophisticated jokes, like the presence of a restaurant called Cavern on the Green, in salute to New York City's tourist mecca Tavern on the Green, gave adults something to chuckle at. Steven Spielberg even sent himself up with a credit for Steven Spielrock, thus adding to the endless array of rock jokes in the movie. The box office take for the first weekend was $37.3 million, higher than all but a few blockbuster action films had ever grossed in their opening days, and the movie kept right on pulling in audiences through the summer months. Asked by Harry Smith of *CBS This Morning* in October 1994 how much *The Flintstones* had made, Rosie cheerily replied, "Three hundred billion." The actual figure was closer to three hundred *million,* including foreign and video rentals, but that made it one of the top-grossing comedies of all time. What's more, Rosie's Betty Rubble laugh had endeared her to millions of movie patrons and caused many critics to say she was the best thing in it. As *Village Voice* critic Joe Levy put it, ". . . Rosie O'Donnell's triumph cannot be overstated (she *sounds* like Betty Rubble, she *actually sounds* like Betty Rubble . . .)." In addition the "Happy Meal" figure of Betty Rubble used in the McDonald's promotion proved to be particularly popular as a collectible, in part because it duplicated the blue band around Rosie's ankle that she wore to hide her tattoo.

Rosie was obviously delighted with the movie's great success, but she wasn't unaware of its shortcomings. Eventually, she would admit that it "could've been funnier," and on another occasion said, "You don't go to *The Flintstones* expecting anything but a cartoon, you know. You go to McDonald's, you get a Big Mac. You go see *The Flintstones,* you get the Flintstones." But she kept these remarks to herself until the movie had finished its run in theaters. When it opened, once again Rosie proved to be terrific at publicity interviews. She was funny, she was charming, and she told great stories about making the movie. Meeting Elizabeth Taylor was an obvious subject, but Rosie could also do a whole riff on driving a Stone Age car: "The car was really scary," she told CBS's Harry Smith in May. "It's basically a golf cart that they added cement wheels to. You know how easy it is to steer cement, Harry. We're going down this slick hill and it's wain—raining. It's wet and Rick [Moranis] looks over at me as we're rolling and he's like, 'We're gonna die. We're gonna die. There's no brakes. We're gonna die.' And I'm like, 'Just keep smiling. We won't have to do it again. Just keep smiling.' We pulled up—we crashed into the curb. It was, like, so scary. The cars were really scary." This little performance by Rosie is an object lesson in how to be funny and seduce the action-movie audience at the same time.

The opening of *The Flintstones* on May 17, 1994, was important to Rosie because it would considerably increase the number of Americans who knew exactly who she was, and who looked forward to seeing her again. However, the previous week something else had happened that meant more to her personally; she had experienced her first opening night as the star of a Broadway musical. That had been the first dream of the little girl from Commack, Long Island, one that her mother had encouraged before her death when Rosie was ten. Television and movies had been a part of the dream, too, but nothing could eclipse the wonder of a Broadway dream come true.

Rosie hadn't seen the original Broadway production of *Grease,* even though it had run for more than seven years, but she had been enthralled with the 1978 movie, which had starred John Travolta, Olivia Newton-John, and Stockard Channing. In those days Stockard Channing had yet to establish herself as one of America's greatest stage actresses, but she had had some success in movies—most notably, playing the female lead opposite Warren Beatty and Jack Nicholson in Mike Nichols's *The Fortune* in 1975. She was already thirty-four when she was cast as Betty Rizzo in *Grease*—seemingly too old to play a teenager—but she had scored a major hit as the leader of the tough girls' gang, the

Pink Ladies, getting the best reviews of anyone in the film. Rosie had been very taken with Channing's performance, and when she heard during the filming of *The Flintstones* that the Tony Award–winning director, choreographer, and performer Tommy Tune was planning a Broadway revival of *Grease,* Rosie immediately determined that she would play Rizzo. Betty Rubble, Betty Rizzo!

Agents hate it when movie actors decide that they want to do a play. For one thing, the difference in pay for the actor can amount to several hundred thousand or even several million dollars. That also cuts deeply into the agents' income, which is based on a percentage of earnings. They also argue that there is no point in being seen by a few hundred thousand people on Broadway (if the show is a hit) when an actor can be seen by millions in a movie. Rosie heard just such protests from her representative, but she was determined to get the part.

Not only was performing on Broadway one of her great dreams, but Rizzo seemed exactly the right role for her to attempt. As she later told Charles Gibson on *Good Morning America,* "I'm not a singer. Tyne Daly wasn't a singer, Katharine Hepburn wasn't a singer, Lauren Bacall is not a singer. These are all women who've done musicals." In fact Tyne Daly had won the Tony for the 1990 revival of *Gypsy,* Katharine Hepburn had had a long run and been nominated for a Tony for 1981's *Coco,* only to be beaten for the award by Lauren Bacall in that years's *Woman of the Year.* Bacall had also won for *Applause* in 1970. Rosie knew she wasn't going to do a part like fashion designer Coco Chanel, or a svelte sophisticate of the kind played by Lauren Bacall. But an endearing toughie like Rizzo she knew she could do. And, not incidentally, she was still three years younger than Stockard Channing had been when she made the movie.

Her agents were against the move. Her *League of Their Own* pal Tom Hanks, who had started out in the theater, told her she'd be bored stiff doing eight shows a week month after month, and when she contacted Tommy Tune's people they seemed hardly to know who she was. This last was particularly discouraging, and it wouldn't be until later that she was able to put it into perspective, noting that theater people lead lives that are in many ways isolated: "They are working during prime time and during moviegoing time. What do they know?" Rosie was determined that before she got through, they would know about her.

She managed to get an audition in New York for June 21, 1993. There was a break in the filming of *The Flintstones,* and she was scheduled to fly to New York to promote *Sleepless in Seattle* anyway. Rosie, smart as ever about seizing an opportunity, managed to turn an interview with Charles Gibson on *Good Morning America* about *Sleepless* into a "preaudition" for her *Grease* audition, which was to take place that very afternoon. Not only did she announce to Gibson what she was going to be doing in the afternoon—thus taking the risk of being embarrassed if she didn't get the role—she also insisted on singing "Happy Talk" from *South Pacific.*

When she arrived for her audition that afternoon, the *Grease* people were a good deal less hazy about who she was.

Neither Tommy Tune nor the show's director and choreographer, Jeff Calhoun, who had assisted Tune on other shows, had seen Rosie on television that morning, but others on the production team had. The atmosphere was quite different than it might have been without her "Happy Talk" rendition. Rosie sang two songs, lied about her dancing ability, and then launched into a pep talk on how much she could do for the show in terms of selling tickets, based on the great success of *A League of Their Own,* the anticipated success of *Sleepless in Seattle,* and the fact that *The Flintstones* would be released at about the same time *Grease* opened on Broadway after an out-of-town tour. All of this could have seemed pushy or the sign of an out-of-control ego, except that Rosie had them all laughing. She turned her sales pitch into stand-up, and they loved it. "There was just this quality she had," Calhoun would say later.

The theater world is as full of outsize egos as Hollywood is, but Rosie didn't present herself as the greatest talent since Liza Minnelli, she just talked commonsense about what she could bring the show in terms of box-office clout. This was the first time she had really been able to make this argument. A much greater degree of fame was yet to come, but she was now in a position to point to important credits. She was also becoming comfortable with the fact that there were a lot of people across the country who would actually consider seeing something because she was in it, and that after *Sleepless* and *The Flintstones* there would be a lot more.

Rosie got the role of Betty Rizzo. The columnist Liz Smith let the world know that "Rosie's audition was so spectacular that all the other Rizzos were vanquished, and she was offered the role on the spot." Many people around her still thought she was making a mistake. She was hot in Hollywood, and her price was steadily rising. Her *Flintstones* contract guaranteed her more than $3 million if there was a sequel. Rosie dealt with those issues explicitly in a 1994 interview with *Newsday*, noting that when you got hot there was a terrific temptation to do a movie even if the script was lousy because of how much money was being offered. "I thought taking *Grease* for a year would remove the chance for me to do that. It's very hard to turn down that kinda money. You figure, it's three months, what does it matter? It's three million dollars. My God, I could put my nieces through college."

On most movie sets, there is a minimum of rehearsal, since scenes are shot out of sequence and if something isn't working, another take can always be made. There was always a lot of time between takes. Rehearsals for a Broadway show, particularly a musical, are a different kind of experience, involving a great deal of very hard work as the cast seeks to develop a "final take" that can then be repeated live in performance after performance. It was particularly difficult for Rosie. The rest of the cast knew all the arcane terms used for various dance steps, like "step-touch" and "hip together," and could perform them on cue from the choreographer. Rosie had to learn all of them from the ground up, and would later thank the cast publicly many times for helping her learn the ropes. She also worked with a vocal coach to help her with pitch problems and to turn what she sometimes referred to as her "hollering" into a projection of the song through acting.

There were other members of the cast who were fairly well known, including Ricky Paull Goldin from the world of soap opera, who had been cast as Danny Zuko, and Sam Harris, playing Doody, who had been a top winner on *Star Search* in the male vocal category, but Rosie was the show's best-known performer and got special billing in larger type. This could have made for problems if Rosie had pulled a "Hollywood star" act, but of course she did nothing of the kind. As always, the members of the cast soon became devoted to her and did everything they could to help her out. In fact, director Jeff Calhoun brought the ensemble onstage to join Rosie at the end of both her solo numbers, including "There Are Worse Things I Could Do," in order to boost the climactic notes. There was nothing unusual about this; it was an old Broadway trick to bolster stars who were not topnotch singers.

Rosie managed to praise just about everyone in the cast in various interviews once the show began its crosscountry tour, with stops in major East Coast cities like Washington and Boston, midwestern ones like Detroit and Minneapolis, and West Coast appearances in Costa Mesa, California, and Seattle, Washington. She noted how young Katy Grenfell (one of the Heartbeats in the show) helped her with her singing, and how Sandra Purpuro, playing Cha-Cha, guided her in the dance numbers. She played down her own singing abilities while praising the voices of Sam Harris and of Billy Porter, who appeared as Teen Angel. Her best friend in the cast would prove to be Michelle Blakely, who played Patty Simcox; Michelle would remain one of her closest friends through the years to come.

The California stop for the *Grease* tour came at the same time as the annual Academy Awards, making it possible for Rosie to appear for the first time as a presenter on the Oscar show. She gave out the awards for short films, both animated and live action. This was not a major category, but since it involved two awards, she was onstage for several minutes and cracked up the audience by saying, "Look at me, I'm on the Academy Awards. Can you believe it? I've got the dress. I've got the jewels. I've got the breasts. And they all have to be back at midnight." In fact, she looked elegant in a low-cut black gown with a splashy diamond necklace and earrings. Rosie had worked with a number of stars in her movies so far, but that night's roster of presenters was a roll call of the Hollywood elite, including Glenn Close, Sharon Stone, Goldie Hawn, Shirley MacLaine, Emma Thompson, Anthony Hopkins, Harrison Ford, Nicolas Cage, Tom Hanks, Kirk Douglas, Jeremy Irons, Al Pacino, not to mention her own favorite heartthrob, Tom Cruise. Rosie was thrilled to realize another childhood dream by being part of the Oscar show, but she was also delivering on her promise to Tommy Tune and Jeff Calhoun that her presence in the cast of *Grease* would help sell tickets. Her marquee value had already been demonstrated in advance sales for the tour, but there was no question her appearance on the Oscars would help sell the show even more.

The out-of-town critics during the three months that *Grease* spent on the road gave it middling reviews for the most part; there were few pans, and few raves, but always enough good quotes to promote the show. The audience was there anyway, some people going for nostalgia's sake, some for the chance to see Rosie live. *Grease* had never been viewed as a masterpiece of the musical theater, but it had always been an audience pleaser, and was proving to be one again. A number of critics were dubious about Rosie's singing voice (no surprise to her), but most found her funny and appealing, which was all that was needed. Rosie had already inoculated herself against criticism of her singing, saying in many local interviews pretty much what she would say on *CBS This Morning* in April 1994: "If you come to see *Grease* and pay your sixty dollars to sit in the orchestra, you will have a tremendous show vocally, a wonderful theatrical experience. I'm not promising it'll be delivered by me."

Whoever heard that remark knew what they would get from Rosie: some good laughs and a sense of fun. Rosie, they were sure, would give them a good time—and she did. When the show opened in New York in May, the reviews were mixed, as they had been on the road, but the quality that Rosie brought to it was pinpointed by Nancy Franklin in a review in *The New Yorker* on May 30, 1994. "Rosie O'Donnell," she wrote, "making her Broadway debut as the tough-talking Rizzo, is the very soul of likability; she is so game and seems so happy to be part of this enterprise that even though she doesn't project very well, and doesn't have much of a singing voice, you're on her side." Like many critics, Franklin was taken by the sets, costumes, and lighting, wowed by Billy Porter's singing as Teen Angel, and generally felt that the show was a complete success as a "fun fur that's not trying to pass as the real thing," offering nostalgia "with such unembarrassed affection that you willingly go along with its gleeful phoniness."

Rosie had signed for nine months with *Grease,* including a month's rehearsal, three months on the road, and five months in New York. The show that she helped establish was still running three years later in the fall of 1997. Numerous guest stars were brought in to play various roles, including Brooke Shields and Linda Blair in the part of Rizzo, a ploy that kept interest in the show going. Just after Rosie left the show, another new movie of hers would premiere, one that had had people wondering what Rosie was doing in it long before it opened.

A movie based on an erotic novel written under the pseudonym Anne Rampling by famous vampire chronicler Anne Rice?

A part originally intended for the sexy star of *Fatal Instinct,* Sharon Stone?

A role that would require Rosie to spend a good deal of time in a studded black leather corset with garters and fishnet stockings?

Does any of this sound like a movie for Rosie O'Donnell? Wouldn't any one of these aspects of the movie and the role make her think twice—maybe even three times—about taking the job?

But Rosie hadn't even hesitated, because there was one

more important fact outweighing all the others. The movie, called *Exit to Eden,* was to be directed by Garry Marshall. Not only was Marshall the brother of *A League of Their Own* director Penny Marshall, but he had been in that film, playing the owner of the baseball team. The most recent movie he had directed was the hugely popular *Pretty Woman,* which had made a major star of Julia Roberts. As Rosie put it, Marshall had taken "a story about a prostitute who ends up dead in Hollywood and turned it into Cinderella for the eighties." If he could do that with the original *Pretty Woman* script, who was to say he couldn't make something wonderful out of Anne Rice's kinky and explicit novel?

Playing a role that Sharon Stone had dropped out of was not really a drawback in Rosie's mind. She made fun of the whole idea. "And I couldn't imagine that meeting where they say, you know, 'Can't get Mel Gibson, let's get Danny DeVito.' You now, it didn't make sense to me that they would go from Sharon Stone to me," she admitted. In another sense, the idea of replacing Sharon Stone intrigued her—it was, she suggested, almost reason enough to do the role by itself.

Clearly, Garry Marshall's concept of the film had been changing. By the time he had signed Rosie he saw it as a comedy with erotic elements, and believed that Rosie, playing the role of an undercover detective named Sheila Kingston who tracks a jewel thief to an erotic resort, was just the person to help him achieve a fresh synthesis of comedy and sex. He later said, "We were trying something very new and we needed someone with whom the audience could identify to ease them into this slightly kinky, slightly threatening world. Rosie's innocent, but hers is a hip innocence. It helps take the edge off the sex in the movie. Yet, she's still sexy and, for the first time in her career, she even has a romantic thing going."

Rosie had been asked by Penny Marshall to lose weight for *A League of Their Own* and had not succeeded, but she did lose it for Garry Marshall's movie. Knowing the kind of skimpy costume she would wear for much of the film proved a powerful incentive, and she was able to get down to her "low end" weight, which gave her a thirty-two-inch waist, something she hadn't had in a while. Still, during the first day of filming she felt self-conscious in her leather corset. Then the crew started telling her how hot she looked, and Rosie had to admit, "After a while I started strutting around going, 'Yeah, I'm pretty in this, aren't I?' I mean, there are some gorgeous people who aren't ninety pounds." Garry Marshall would say later, "She's also very brave. She was taken aback by having to wear some of the skimpy costumes, but she did. She doesn't worry about how she looks all the time. That can be very refreshing in Hollywood."

The rest of the cast included Dan Ackroyd as Rosie's uptight detective partner, Dana Delany (who had won an Emmy for *China Beach*) as the dominatrix proprietess of the sex-fantasy island resort, Paul Mercurio of *Strictly Ballroom* as the young hunk Delany falls for against her will, Hector Elizondo (who had been in all of Garry Marshall's movies) as the sex therapist–guru owner of the resort, and Stuart Wilson and supermodel Iman as the villains. Sean O'Bryan played the "sex slave" who becomes Rosie's romantic interest in the story. This somewhat oddball cast got on well together, and Rosie even forgave Iman for sending her to the hospital to have stitches in her head as a result of their fight scene.

Although Rosie would say later that she had had a wonderful time making the movie, and would make another with Garry Marshall in a minute—even *Exit to Eden II*—because she adored him, she was not very surprised when it turned out to be the kind of box-office flop that critics keep a set of specially sharpened knives in reserve for. On the whole, Rosie didn't get as badly slammed as most of the cast did. There was a reason. Not only did she have most of the best lines and do a surprising amount with them, but she did look sexy in her black leather corset. It was such a different image of Rosie O'Donnell that critics were somewhat disarmed. And the general public, even though it stayed away from the movie in droves, did get to see her in her corset, thanks to a considerable ad campaign, and appeared to think she looked pretty cool. The careers of Garry Marshall and Dana Delany may well have been set back by the movie, but it didn't do Rosie any harm to be seen in such a different light.

In fact, the movie isn't nearly as bad as some that received much better reviews in 1994. The story doesn't really work, since the sex parts and the comedy parts tend to undermine each other, but some of it is funny, and some of it is sexy, and some of it is actually quite sweet. Rosie has some boffo moments. When the "sex slave" who is falling for her asks how he can fulfill her fantasy and she replies, "Go paint my house," this is an example of Rosie O'Donnell's way with a quick retort at its very best. It's impossible not to laugh at many such lines, delivered with her customary snap and good humor.

All in all, 1994 had been very good to Rosie. In *The Flintstones,* she had had her biggest commercial hit yet. She had proved that she could put theatergoers in the seats for *Grease* and she had fulfilled a lifetime ambition to be on Broadway. And even though *Exit to Eden* had been a commercial and critical bomb, she had personally come out of it not only unscathed, but had broadened the public and professional view of her range as a performer.

When a flop movie does you more good than harm, you know you must be doing something right.

SIX

In Demand

By the summer of 1994, when she was starring on Broadway in *Grease,* Rosie had reached a point in her career where it was not going to be possible to do everything that was offered to her. Any actor cherishes that moment, but it is also a juncture when it is almost inevitable that the performer will start making mistakes. This is not necessarily because a newly inflated ego drives the performer always to look for the largest role in the showiest project. Certainly that was not the case with Rosie. In spite of her lead roles in *Another Stakeout* and *Exit to Eden,* she still regarded herself as primarily a character actress. The problem for the actor faced with a choice of roles is that it is extremely difficult for even the most experienced performer, whether on the stage, on television, or in the movies, to tell what will happen to a given project. A role may look wonderful on paper, but by the time the actor is in front of the camera, the part may have been enhanced or downgraded because of script changes made to satisfy the producers, the director, or another star actor. Even if the role remains pretty much as it was in the script that persuaded the actor to sign on, the casting of the rest of the movie, the eventual budget, and many kinds of unforeseen circumstances may play havoc with the making of the movie. No one starts out to make a flop, whether it costs a modest $20 million or today's more usual $70 million. Yet flops are as common as weeds, even if they may have originally looked like rosebushes.

In the summer of 1993, for example, Rosie was offered a role in the latest Hugh Grant vehicle. She would have played a woman with numerous children who befriends Grant's pregnant girlfriend when he gets cold feet about becoming a father. The role of her husband in the eventual movie was played by Tom Arnold, in one of his best performances yet. Perhaps exactly because she had so often been mistaken for Arnold's real-life former wife, Roseanne, Rosie turned the part down and Joan Cusack was cast instead. The movie turned out to be a solid hit, even though it came out soon after Grant's Hollywood arrest in the company of a prostitute in a parked car.

The movie Rosie chose to do instead would have a far more modest degree of success at the box office. *Now and Then* may well have seemed more appealing to her as a script and as a project she felt she would be happy to work on. For one thing, the movie was to be directed by a woman, Lesli Linka Glatter, a situation Rosie had found very comfortable when she worked on *A League of Their Own* with

Penny Marshall, and on *Sleepless in Seattle* with Nora Ephron. The movie was the first to be produced by Demi Moore's own company. Moore would also be one of the adult stars, together with Melanie Griffith and Rosie's friend Rita Wilson, Tom Hanks' wife. These three actresses and Rosie were to play the grown-up women that four girls, the focus of the central portion of the movie, became.

Although set in Indiana, *Now and Then* was to be filmed near Savannah, Georgia, a lovely city then being celebrated in John Berendt's nonfiction (but very novelistic) best-seller, *Midnight in the Garden of Good and Evil,* which would still be on the best-selling list more than three years later. One of the characters in Berendt's book was a transvestite singer named The Lady Chablis, who would go on to play herself in the 1997 movie, based on the book, directed by Clint Eastwood. Rosie and her co-stars, together with Demi Moore's visiting husband, Bruce Willis, went to see The Lady Chablis perform at a Savanah bar. Rosie's years traveling the country doing stand-up, as well as her New York City showbiz background, left her less than dazzled by this experience. "I've seen the best of them," she recalled. "It wasn't exactly the highlight of my trip. Melanie was a bit startled. I don't know how many drag bars she's been to. Rita rolls with the punches. Demi's fascination with the whole thing was more entertaining to me than the drag queens."

In the script for *Now and Then,* it was crystal clear that the character played as a teenager by Christina Ricci and by Rosie as an adult was a lesbian. The adult character is a physician who is thinking of adopting a child with her lady friend, and Rosie liked the fact that this lesbian character was presented as a beloved local doctor, saying "something interesting about how people are accepting of one another." However, dialogue was changed during the looping process, supposedly because the original dialogue would have confused the audience, but the result was another one of Hollywood's "gay with a wink" fudgings of the issue, as had happened with *Fried Green Tomatoes* (1991) and many other movies. Even with women at the helm, Hollywood remained skittish about gay characters.

Some of the critics took note of the "wink" going on here, and few had much good to say about the film as a whole, although they liked the performances by the young actresses who had most of the screen time. Moreover, this had been an inexpensive movie, and did moderately well at the box office.

Another movie that Rosie was brought in to give an injection of energy and humor to was *Beautiful Girls,* eventually released in 1996. This was a mixture of such earlier movies as *The Big Chill* (1983) and *Diner* (1982), combined with the close-knit small-city feeling of *The Deer Hunter* (1978), which director Ted Demme, a nephew of *Silence of the Lambs* (1991) director Jonathan Demme, screened for the cast when they gathered on location in Stillwater, Minnesota. The director was perhaps a little too open about such antecedents, for the critics would complain that the movie was too derivative and failed to live up to its models. They did, however, approve of an interesting, offbeat cast that had been carefully matched to the movie's roles. Among its cast were Matt Dillon, Timothy Hutton, Uma Thurman, Annabeth Gish, Lauren Holly, Martha Plimpton, and Mira Sorvino, who would win a Best Supporting Actress Oscar before the *Beautiful Girls* was released for her performance in Woody Allen's rueful 1995 comedy, *Mighty Aphrodite*.

If the movie was a critical and box office disappointment overall, it did bring Rosie the best reviews of her career. The plot, such as it was, revolved around people returning for their tenth high school reunion. Rosie played a single beauty parlor owner who has stayed in town. Her character, Gina, has given up on men and delivers an extremely funny but blistering scolding to the characters played by Dillon and Hutton on the subject of the women pictured in magazines like *Playboy* and *Penthouse*. It was for this very speech that director Demme had especially wanted Rosie, and she tore into it with a vehemence that elevated the film to another level. And the critics took notice, even those who had no use for the movie. They said that she was "the link holding this amazing cast together," that she offered "an exuberantly profane guide to real women," and that she had delivered an "applause worthy tirade." In fact, Rosie herself experienced that reaction effect when she went to see the movie with her sister Maureen in a New Jersey multiplex: "The women stood up and cheered," she reported. "There was this huge uprising among these overweight, imperfect women."

In this famous speech, Rosie managed to fuse her standup technique with an acting portrayal that struck deep for a great many women, and left many men as astonished as the characters played by Dillon and Hutton. At the same time, Rosie's experiences in the film world were providing terrific material for her ongoing stand-up career. Whether she was imitating with affectionate derision the voices of her friends Demi Moore and Melanie Griffith, or reporting on the agonies suffered by director Ted Demme over the lack of snow in Minnesota, Rosie was finding ways to turn her new life as a movie actress and celebrity into fodder for her stand-up routines. Like Robin Williams, she had decided that a movie career was not going to be the only string to her bow, and kept right on doing engagements as a comic.

By this time, however, Rosie was a major headliner, a star whom people would go see in top venues just for herself. She had much enjoyed her days as an opening act for Dolly Parton and others, but now she was getting top billing. During late 1994 and early 1995, she appeared at a number of smaller clubs to try out material for an HBO special she was developing, which was to be taped in April 1995. Not only had she been busy with movies, but her long stint on VH-1 had involved only short takes. She knew it was necessary to get her edge back before live audiences and to build the kind of longer act that would be necessary for the HBO special. One of the sequences of this act involved what it felt like to make the transformation from fan to star. As she told the press in Chicago in early spring 1995, where she was appearing with her new club act, "As much as I've achieved some sort of success in the film industry, I don't feel any different. And I think people have this illusion, including myself before it happened to me, that everything was going to change once you sort of made it." She noted that ". . . you become friends with who you work with, because that's life. But it's really no different than if I got a job at the high school teaching English, and I was hanging out with the art teacher and the janitor." She was prepared to admit that there were perks that went with her new life, like flying first class, and that life was much less lonely than when she'd been driving from gig to gig and "staying at Motel 6."

• • •

Comedy is a combative art form. If you're not trained and you go into the boxing ring, you're gonna get the crap kicked out of you. The audience is ready—they know you can deliver a good punch, so they're waiting for that punch—and if you don't have it, you're gonna get beat up.

Rosie O'Donnell, in early 1995, on getting back into top shape as a stand-up comic

• • •

The press has always been reluctant to accept the idea that a star's life doesn't change the basic person, and certainly many stars seem to change a lot, becoming prima donnas overnight. What perhaps both sides ignore is that people who get to be stars are seldom really "ordinary" in the first place. Yet, if anyone has a right to claim that she hasn't changed all that much it is Rosie O'Donnell. In fact, it is the connection she retains with the realities of her audiences and viewers that is a large part of her appeal.

The HBO special was taped, at Rosie's request, at the Comedy Connection in Boston. It was one of her favorite clubs and had its own special connection to the past. Back in 1982, she had been bundled into a car at the Comedy Connection and sent off to Plums in Worchester, Massachusetts, where she earned her first $60 on the professional circuit. Of course, the audience for her taping was willing to cheer her on no matter what, but they got the terrific show they had hoped for. The show mixed her usual self-deprecating stories about herself and her adventures with sharp contemporary commentary, including a telling joke about the guilt of O. J. Simpson, one of the few people she has attacked head-on during her career.

Not only did the HBO special score with her fans across the country, it brought her her first Emmy nomination. She was nominated for Outstanding Individual Performance in a Variety or Music Program. A nomination was a great step forward in itself, but Rosie was perhaps most thrilled that her childhood idol Barbra Streisand was competing against her in the same category for her own musical special, the famous Las Vegas show that had also appeared on HBO and been released as a video. Barbra won, as expected, but for Rosie just having her name read out along with Streisand's must have seemed like a dream come true for the fan from Commack.

Rosie was popping up all over television in the period

between her Broadway run in *Grease* and the debut of her own show a year and a half later. There had been a guest appearance on the sitcom *Bless This House* during it's brief run. Fran Drescher, whom Rosie had known since stand-up days, asked Rosie to do a cameo on *The Nanny* as an aggressive New York cab driver, and Rosie had responded with hilarious results to this bit of typecasting. Her friendship with Drescher was such that she got to know Fran's parents very well, and later had the bright idea of asking them to appear on *The Rosie O'Donnell Show,* giving tips from their Florida home on restaurants, movies, and other subjects. As had always been the case, the events of Rosie's life seemed naturally to give rise to new possibilities. She had a true gift for friendship, and for making people glad they knew her, going all the way back to her prom queen days at Commack High. Now that gift was paying dividends in a far more competitive and sophisticated world.

Another relationship that would involve a considerable amount of professional give-and-take developed with David Letterman. She and Letterman were not exactly pals—he wasn't given to easy showbiz camaraderie—but they respected each other and helped one another out on several occasions. She had first appeared on *Late Night with David Letterman* on January 5, 1994. Even Letterman's rather tough "seen it all" staff would comment later on the rousing success of that first appearance. Once Rosie relocated from Los Angeles to New York, she became one of the people whom Letterman counted on as a last-minute fill-in for guests who suddenly canceled an appearance. Television viewers are acutely aware that scheduled guests—especially young singers or comics who are not very well known—sometimes get bumped from a show because another more important guest has talked too long. It used to happen all too frequently with Johnny Carson, and viewers always felt sorry for the guest who didn't get to appear. There is another side to this coin; guests who drop out and leave a gaping hole in the day's taping. Letterman found that Rosie was capable of coming on at very short notice and doing a terrific job.

. . .

Hi David, it's Rosie—
read the wire, we're on fire,
do you think you could lend us a hand?
Hey Rosie, it's David—
do a great show, from the Late Show,
need a place? Use my space.
I'm so glad I could lend you a hand.

Lyrics sung by Rosie O'Donnell, to the tune of the telephone song from *Bye Bye Birdie*, on her first broadcast from David Letterman's studio, in October 1996

. . .

Thus Rosie was one of the stars Letterman called on to tape an "audition" for the fake movie he featured as an inside joke during his disastrous turn at hosting the Oscars in

Rosie's TV credits range from one of her early shows, *Gimme a Break (above)*—in which she appeared with Joey *(center)* and Matthew Lawrence—to her current superstardom as host of her own talk show *(below)*.

Rosie has played roles on the silver screen in such major films as *The Flintstones (left)*, *Sleepless in Seattle (below)* with Meg Ryan, and *A League of Their Own (bottom)* with Madonna.

On camera and off, Rosie hobnobs with such stars as Tom Cruise *(above),* her biggest crush, and Oprah *(below),* the "other" queen of daytime talk.

These days, with an award-winning talk show and tons of fans, everything's coming up Rosie! Rosie accepts an Emmy for her show in 1997 *(above)* and appears with a group of look-alikes *(below)*.

1995. Of all the stars who appeared on this silly sequence, Rosie got the biggest laugh by using a bleeped obscenity that summed up the inane antics all too well. Her appearances on his talk show had more lasting and positive results in that she would ultimately hire two of his top people to work on her own show in 1996. Daniel Kellison, a segment producer for Letterman, moved over to *The Rosie O'Donnell Show* as executive producer, and Randy Cohen would become her head writer. Letterman took the loss of his two staff members with grace. In fact, when Rosie's studio, along with many others at Rockefeller Center, was put out of commission on October 10, 1996, Letterman, who was on a week's break, allowed Rosie to use his CBS theater on Broadway, which had once been the home to *The Ed Sullivan Show*.

David Letterman wasn't the only person to realize that Rosie could fill in successfully for a missing celebrity. George Burns had been scheduled to make an appearance for his one hundredth birthday at Caesar's Palace in Las Vegas, Nevada, in January 1996. He was not well enough to keep this much publicized date, however, and Rosie was asked to take his place. This was a considerable tribute to Rosie's standing in show business, and a far cry from her first appearance in Las Vegas as an opening act years earlier, when she had been told off for running over her allotted time by a minute or two. Rosie had played Las Vegas many times since, most recently as the headliner at the MGM Grand in November 1995. But to be asked to take over for a legend like George Burns was a special event.

Burns himself called her backstage during her engagement at Caesar's Palace. They had never met or spoken to each other before, but he talked shop with her about how her new television show, which would start in June, was selling in various markets. On the spur of the moment she invited him to appear on her first show, telling him what an honor that would be for her. His reply was, "I don't know, sweetheart. I'll try to do it. But I gotta go see Gracie." He was referring of course to his late wife Gracie Allen, who had played the hilariously confused partner to his straight man on vaudeville stages, in Hollywood musicals, and on radio and television. After her death Burns had wondered how he could go on without her, but eventually he found an entirely new career on his own, not only in Las Vegas and on television, but in a number of hit movies including the *Oh, God!* series starting in 1977. He had also won the Oscar for Best Supporting Actor for *The Sunshine Boys* (1976). Burns was not only show business royalty, but also an example of how far a stand-up comic could go, and Rosie was thrilled by their conversation and touched by the fact that he had taken the trouble to call her in the midst of his illness. She later paid touching tribute to him, recalling their conversation and his death not long after, on March 9, 1996, saying, "Well, he didn't make our show; but he did keep his date with Gracie. And maybe he did make the show after all. I'd like to think so."

Rosie wasn't show business royalty yet, but she was on her way. An indication of how far she'd come was that she was asked to host *Catch a Rising Star's 50th Anniversary*—

Give or Take 26 Years on TV. This CBS special looked back on the saga of the Manhattan comedy club where so many of the famous comics now starring in sitcoms and movies had performed in earlier days, including Rosie herself. She was now among the best known of them, someone whose name could get people to tune in to a television special, put people in the seats for a Broadway musical, and give them an extra reason to go see a new movie.

Perhaps the surest measure of her status was the series of very funny TV commercials she made for Kmart with Penny Marshall, which began appearing in November 1995. Although Marshall was now a major Hollywood director, the public fondly remembered her days as the co-star of *Laverne and Shirley.* The Kmart commercials, with ten scripts written by Rosie, had Penny and Rosie shopping at Kmart in *Laverne and Shirley* style, with Rosie helping to interpret Marshall's famous New York mumble. The friendship between Rosie and Penny, which had flourished since Penny plucked Rosie off VH-1 to co-star in *A League of Their Own,* gave the commercials a wonderfully relaxed feel, and Rosie's scripts were perfectly tailored to the two women's personalities. They were a hugely successful marketing ploy for Kmart, and caused several critics to call them more fun than some of the shows the spots were placed on. The commercials didn't just make Rosie a great deal of money, reportedly as much as $1 million, they also created new Rosie O'Donnell fans across the country, a signal achievement for any commercial. In still another show business arena, Rosie had hit the bull's-eye.

SEVEN

Adopting a Son Named Parker

In the 1980s, single-parent adoptions increased. At the same time, new scientific developments made it possible for some couples to take a new route to childbirth, making use of fertility drugs, artificial insemination, and surrogate mothers. It was in this climate, which offered many different routes to parenthood, that Rosie O'Donnell decided to adopt a child in 1994.

Rosie considered all the options, getting advice from several friends who had adopted. She had quickly ruled out artificial insemination, which she regarded as a "freaky concept," adding with typical Rosie humor, "I don't want to have coffee with a stranger." She also said that she had "no ego investment in re-creating myself." In addition, she thought it was perhaps wise not to "dive into my gene pool and go fishing, because there's a tremendous amount of illness in my family, a tremendous amount of alcoholism."

That had not stopped her sister Maureen from having children, or her brothers, but Rosie was perhaps more sensitive to the problems in the family medical history than her siblings, since her mother's death from cancer at such a young age had hit her so hard.

• • •

I always knew I would have children. It was never a question. Just as I knew what I wanted for my career, I knew I would be a mother. And though I was not against being a birth mother, this opportunity came up. I knew people who had adopted, so I put myself on a list, like throwing a wish into the air. I thought, if this is meant to be then it will happen.

Rosie O'Donnell in *Good Housekeeping,* June 1997

• • •

And so Rosie contacted a Los Angeles lawyer recommended by friends. "I filled out the papers, I was fingerprinted, and I waited," she said. The wait was less than a year. Her son was born premature, at only seven months, and when Rosie saw a photograph of him taken just after his birth, she was somewhat unnerved. She called her sister Maureen on the East Coast and said, "My son is a smooshed-up tomato, all red and blotchy." But Maureen reassured her: "All babies look like that."

She decided to call her son Parker Jaren O'Donnell. Her

choice of a first name she explained to the press thus: "With a name like Parker he can grow up to be either a surfer or a Supreme Court justice." The Jaren was chosen because it provided a family connection. "When my brother Timmy was little we called him T.J., and in fact all the males in my family have the middle initial J. My dad's Edward J., my brothers, Eddie J., Danny J. and Timmy J., and so Parker J." She emphasized that she expected her brothers to provide a male parenting influence in her son's life.

More information about the choice of the name Parker developed when Kirstie Alley appeared on Rosie's show nearly a year later. Perhaps she was simply trying to establish rapport with Alley, but she told her, "My son is kinda named after your husband—Parker Stevenson—I liked the *Hardy Boys* as a kid and I decided back then if I ever had a baby boy I would name him Parker." She has admitted to calling him "Boo-Boo" and "Boo-Bear," among other nicknames, adding, "Do you think he'll need therapy?" On the air she often also refers to him, as she does many children and even some adults, as a "cutie-patootie."

Rosie was exceptionally honest with the media about the adoption process, revealing to *Life, Good Housekeeping,* and to Katie Couric on MSNBC that the process had been easier for her than for most people. "I was lucky," she told *Good Housekeeping.* "Celebrity affords many luxuries in our society. These are the sad truths of our culture." To *Life,* she admitted, "You're given privileges whether you want them or not. I'm very conscious that most people wait much longer to adopt. But you wouldn't say, 'No thanks, I don't want that baby.' I think you get the child you're supposed to have in your life." "It's not like I didn't have to go through the process," she told Couric, "but to deny that who I am didn't help things along would be a lie. The truth is, having money helps in every situation. The price of stardom is a loss of privacy. But aside from that, the money that comes with stardom makes life easier in every other way. I can't deny that."

Her conversation with Katie Couric on *Internight,* Couric's MSNBC program, brought an approving comment from columnist Liz Smith. Smith wrote that she had heard the question about the speed of the process being asked other celebrities, "and the answer is always, 'Oh, no, we had to wait like anybody else.'" Smith then repeated Rosie's frank reply to Couric. Rosie's honesty on this subject is clearly genuine—but it also helps her maintain the special connection to her fans that makes her an unusual entertainment figure. Most celebrities like to pretend that they're not that different from other people, but by admitting that in some ways she inevitably is different serves to endear Rosie to her audience. Americans don't necessarily begrudge other people's great success—after all, that's the American dream—but they are pleasantly surprised when someone with that kind of good fortune is willing to admit that it does indeed carry certain privileges.

Rosie told interviewers that she had always known she would have children, that "not having a mom growing up, I knew children would be my priority." But although she'd had a lot of experience in helping to raise her two younger siblings after her mother's death, she had never before dealt with a baby. She was launched into motherhood with a baby shower given by *Sleepless in Seattle* star and good friend Meg Ryan, a party that was attended by Geena Davis and Carrie Fisher, among others. She also needed some more practical advice, and here two of her other actress friends provided particular help.

Kate Capshaw, the wife of Steven Spielberg and a busy mother herself, was given particular credit by Rosie. "She provided everything I needed in any way, shape, or form. During the first three months, I thought she should establish 1-800-CALL KATE for new mothers. You'd say anything to her, like 'I don't think these are the right-size diapers,' and suddenly you'd hear beep-beep-beep and a truck would be pulling up. And a delivery man would say, 'Here's 95,000 diapers from Ms. Capshaw.' " Capshaw even arranged for Parker to be circumcised. Rosie thought that had been carried out at the hospital in Florida where he was born, but she didn't think he *looked* as though he'd been circumcised. "I thought maybe there was some genital configuration that changes at puberty. I didn't know." So she got Kate Capshaw to take a look. Capshaw confirmed that the procedure hadn't been carried out and arranged for the head of the OB-GYN unit at Cedars-Sinai in Los Angeles to do the job. What's more, this physician had official Jewish religious authority to perform the *bris,* as it is called, so that it became a traditional ceremony and not just a surgical procedure.

Rosie was also worried about the baby's feeding, which brought Tom Hanks's wife, actress Rita Wilson, over with her own mother in tow. Rosie was terrified because Parker wouldn't eat. "But Rita's mother got him to drink a whole bottle. I kept saying how nervous I was, and she's from Greece, and she said, 'Rosie, they throw babies in the trash bin and they live for days. You can't kill him! Don't worry.'" This blunt way of putting it—so like something Rosie herself might say in an irreverent moment—helped put the new mother at ease.

For the first few months, Rosie concentrated on her new son. However, it was also necessary to provide for them financially, so Rosie took Parker off with her to Toronto to film *Harriet the Spy* in the fall of 1995. Rosie was delighted to be doing this movie, since the 1973 book had been one of her favorites as a child. Louise Fitzhugh's story revolves around a young girl who wants to be a writer, and thus spies on everyone she knows to gather material. But the journal she keeps of her findings is discovered, causing a good deal of horror and outrage among those she has been observing. Her aspirations are defended by a nanny called Golly, and it was this role that Rosie had been asked to play. The movie was the first feature produced by the cable channel Nickelodeon, and they had cast the star of one of their own children's shows, *The Adventures of Pete and Pete,* ten-year-old Michelle Trachtenberg, to play Harriet. Rosie would get second billing, although the role of Golly was not particularly large. It was a project Rosie was happy to be part of not only because she knew and cherished the book, but also because, as she pointed out, "it encourages young girls to be independent and artistic and intellectual and strong." She recalled that the book had even inspired her to spy on her brothers and keep a diary. To avoid Harriet's problems, Rosie kept her diary in code, and she couldn't even "understand it when I found it twenty years later." When she subsequently did publicity for the movie, she was asked if she still spied on people. Rosie had to admit that she did, but gave the confession a typical New York twist, reflecting her move back to the city from California: "I live in New York City and I do have binoculars near my window. Sometimes I look across the street, and I see other people looking at me with their binoculars."

Rosie had in part been chosen for the role because she had won the Favorite Actress award voted by the kids who watched Nickelodeon in the most recent poll, a victory based on her performance as Betty Rubble in *The Flintstones*.

• • •

I want to tell you—all you kids here and all you kids at home—that you can live your dreams if you keep believing in yourself. So keep believing, and thank you very much.

Rosie O'Donnell, accepting the Nickelodeon Kids' Choice Award,
May 1995

• • •

Rosie enjoyed the shoot, and all the kids on the set, helping to keep them entertained as she had the adults on other movie sets. She even got into a cherry pit–spitting contest with Michelle Trachtenberg, which Michelle admitted Rosie won. But the time playing with the children acting in the movie only made Rosie more aware that she and Parker were not together. Even though he was with her in Toronto, the long days of shooting meant that she got to see him only about an hour a day when he was awake.

When *Harriet the Spy* was released the following July, it garnered mixed reviews, some quite enthusiastic but others suggesting it didn't quite jell. It did do fairly well at the box office, taking in more than $25 million, and would subsequently fare well on video. Rosie got a good deal of the credit for that, and reviewers who liked the movie as a whole also tended to praise Rosie's performance. The new mother must have particularly liked several reviews that viewed her Golly as the kind of wise but humorous adult any child would want in his or her life. However, when she was making the movie, Rosie was keenly aware of the need to change her mode of work to make it possible to be central to her own child's life.

By the end of the shooting schedule, Rosie was publicly musing about this problem, but she still had other commitments to honor. Fortunately, both were small roles that did not require an extended shoot for her. First she appeared as a nun who teaches the central character in *Wide Awake,* about a ten-year-old boy looking for the meaning of God after his grandfather's death. Once again, she got to play baseball in a movie, and was reunited with Dana Delany (as the boy's mother), both of them playing roles at the opposite end of the spectrum from those they had in *Exit to Eden*.

Rosie then undertook another brassy comic role in *The Twilight of the Golds*, based on the Broadway play of 1993 by Jonathan Tolin, and produced for the cable channel Showtime. This movie was about whether a woman should bring to term a baby whom genetic testing has shown likely to be homosexual like her brother—played out as a comedy about a neurotic Jewish family of means. It had not been a hit on Broadway, and it would receive mixed reviews on television, but Rosie got to work with a cast that included Faye Dunaway as the prospective grandmother, Jennifer Beals as her pregnant daughter who must decide whether or not to have an abortion, and, in minor roles, Jack Klugman (famous for *The Odd Couple*) and Phyllis Frelich, the deaf actress who had won a Tony for the central role in the Broadway production of *Children of a Lesser God* (for which Marlee Matlin would win an Oscar in the film version). Also on board were old friend Garry Marshall, acting rather than directing, and Rosie's close friend from *Grease*, Michelle Blakely. Rosie's role as an infertile co-worker of Beals's was a small juicy one of the sort she could now toss off in her sleep.

During this period, Rosie also had a cameo part in *A Very Brady Sequel*. But the presence of Parker in her life was about to take her career in an entirely new direction as she sought to integrate him more successfully into her working life. In the meantime, she was enjoying her role as mother every bit as much as she had expected. She would later sum up what he meant to her in an interview with *Good Housekeeping:* "It's been very, very healing for me. For the first time, I can perceive my mother as an adult. Because my mom died when I was a kid, my images of her were always idealized. I never really saw her as a woman. But when I first held my son in my arms, I had that overwhelming connection and a feeling of immense love that I never had before. I thought, *My mother felt this for me. And for my siblings.* So it was a really emotional time for me, those first few months with Parker, to connect with my mom and to think of her as a woman and not as my little girl's image of her."

. . .

We're working on, like "Touch Mommy's nose." That's what we're working on this week. But he's just discovered he can use his hands . . . every day he makes a new discovery. And I hate to sound like all those people that I used to watch on TV and go, "Oh, will you shut up about your kids." But here I am, going "You know what? Yesterday he got all the rice cereal in his mouth," you know. But it is a life-altering experience. You literally grow another heart, and sort of the world has more colors, and it's the best thing I ever did.

Rosie O'Donnell to Charles Gibson, on *Good Morning America,* November 1995

. . .

EIGHT

The Rosie O'Donnell Show

The April 1994 issue of *Glamour* contained an article by Charla Krupp headed WHEN WILL A WOMAN HOST A LATE-NIGHT TALK SHOW? It noted that 55 percent of late-night viewers were women, but that all the talk show hosts were men. Krupp assembled a list of women who she felt had what it took to host such a show. The list included some famous names like Cher and Lily Tomlin, actresses with a comic style, such as Teri Garr, Fran Drescher, and Kathy Najimy, as well as Paula Poundstone, the stand-up comic, Robin Quivers of the Howard Stern radio show, and the multifaceted Tracey Ullman. At the very top of the list was Rosie O'Donnell. What's more, a drawing at the head of the article showed Rosie as a host, complete with her own name coffee cup, together with "dream" guests Roseanne Arnold, Cher, and Bette Midler.

When Krupp interviewed Rosie for the article, Rosie told

her that she had in fact been offered the time period that Chevy Chase had briefly held in his disastrous foray into late-night television, and that Buena Vista Television had suggested that she do a syndicated late-night show. There had even been some talk with NBC about taking over for Bob Costas. At that time Rosie simply wasn't interested in the idea. She was about to make *The Flintstones,* and told Krupp, "I just started this acting thing, and it's going so well that I'm not going to fold the hand yet."

With the adoption of Parker her attitude would change. A late-night show, which would have to be taped in the evening even if it didn't go out live, was clearly not the answer. That would keep her away from Parker during the supper and bedtime hours. What's more, in spite of her sassy humor and background in stand-up comedy that was angled toward the nighttime club crowd, Rosie had a hunch she would really be better suited to a daytime show. She had had some experience with both kinds of shows. In the first week of August 1993, she had filled in one day for Kathie Lee on the syndicated daytime show *Live with Regis and Kathie Lee,* and in mid-June 1995 she had been the substitute host for NBC's *Later with Greg Kinnear.* Then in the early fall of 1995 she had substituted for Kathie Lee Gifford again. It was the latter experience that would make up her mind what she wanted to do.

As she would later tell several interviewers, she was forcefully struck by the time involved in doing the show with Regis Philbin. "I arrived there at 8:45 A.M. and got home at 10:20 A.M." Of course, since Rosie was just filling in, she didn't have to go through any of the time-consuming off-camera work that goes into a talk show. She knew what that could entail from her long stint as both producer and on-air host of *Stand-up Spotlight* on VH-1. She was also aware that Kathie Lee Gifford had brought her own young children with her to work, and had them close by in a specially arranged nursery at the studio. She thought such an arrangement would make it possible to spend the amount of time she wanted with Parker, and extend her career in a new direction as well.

Rosie had heard Kathie Lee make noises about possibly leaving her show, and asked her agent to put Rosie forward as a replacement if that should happen. "My agent said, 'You don't want to do that. Are you crazy?' I said, 'No, I really want to do it; it's a great gig. It's fun, it's interesting, you get to talk to celebrities.' " Her agent had a better idea: Why not see if somebody would give Rosie her own show? That sounded great to Rosie, but she made it clear even at that early stage that she didn't want to do something "depressing, like Ricki Lake and the guy who slept with the mother's father or whatever."

Chatting up celebrities on television had a history almost as old as the medium, but it became a national phenomenon on NBC in the early 1950s when Pat Weaver, father of movie star Sigourney Weaver, created first the *Today* show and then *Tonight!*, launched in September 1954 with Steve Allen as host. Allen's three-year tenure was followed by that of Jack Parr, and then Johnny Carson took over in 1962 and ruled the late-night airwaves for thirty years. Copycat shows came and went, and more easygoing versions, starring Mike Douglas, Merv Griffin, and Dinah Shore, had successful daytime runs. Rosie had grown up with these daytime stalwarts, and it was their brand of pleasant good humor that she wanted to emulate, with a little David Letterman/ Jay Leno hipness thrown in.

What she didn't want to do was a discussion show, with hot-button social subjects and confessional antics. These formats had a respectable lineage, from Phil Donahue's daytime show and David Susskind's more intellectual evening program, whose interest to viewers had been confirmed with the great success of Oprah Winfrey. However, daytime shows in the 1990s had become more and more sensationalistic, many of them featuring supposedly "ordinary" Americans who told pathetic and horrifying tales of incest, drug addiction, and murderous feuds. Some of these guests were clearly deranged, others laughingly inept, although it was difficult not to feel sorry for them as word leaked out that they were being flown into town and met by limousines, only to be shipped out by bus. One of Geraldo Rivera's shows actually degenerated into on-air violence, while Jenny Jones found herself in the middle of a murder case involving the on-air admission by one guest that he had a homosexual crush on another, who subsequently shot and killed his admirer.

These shows were being labeled "trash TV" by the mid-1990s, and editorialists and politicians were having a field day condemning daytime television as "degenerate," and a threat to "the moral fabric of the nation." What's more, many of the newer shows of this sort were disappearing without a trace after a few months of dismal ratings. The time was right for something different. So once again, Rosie O'Donnell's timing was perfect. Just as she had gotten into stand-up as new clubs were opening all across the country and female comics were gaining new respect, just as she had been in exactly the right place to land her roles in *A League of Their Own* and *Sleepless in Seattle,* so were her talent and her personality precisely suited to daytime television's need for a fresher, nicer show.

. . .

You know, there's a mentality, Sally, not just with Andrew Dice Clay, with a lot of comedians, that it doesn't matter what you say, as long as they laugh. That the fact that someone laughs justifies the hateful, hurtful comments that you make. And I don't think that's a valid reason. The end does not justify the means. And just because he's selling out Madison Square Garden doesn't mean that he's going to be around forever. . . .

Rosie O'Donnell to Sally Jessy Raphaël, July 1990

. . .

Selling Rosie to television producers proved to be almost absurdly easy. She was a movie actress who had had crucial roles in several major hits, she was a nationally known stand-up comic with a comedy club following across the country who had produced her own cable show for years, she had scored with an HBO special and a Radio City Music Hall New Year's Eve show, she'd just finished starring in a hit Broadway musical and, not least, she was known in the business as one of the best promoters of her vehicles going, someone both print and television journalists loved to interview. On top of that, her concept for a show that would revive the friendly, amusing atmosphere generated by Mike Douglas and Dinah Shore seemed the perfect antidote to all the "trash TV" discussions taking place in the political arena.

It was not so much a matter of selling Rosie to producers as playing them off against one another to get the best possible deal. Sony, Disney, King World, and Rysher Entertainment, among others, courted her. She went with Warner Brothers, even though reportedly, Warner did not offer her the most money. Rosie looked at all the angles, and decided that Warner had the best record in terms of commitment and willingness to make changes when necessary on the basis of other shows they had handled. Not that Warner's monetary offer was in any way paltry—industry analysts put it at about $4.5 million for the first year, plus a share of profits through the participation of her own Kid Ro Entertainment Company. Warner got her the 175-seat New York studio in Rockefeller Center once used by Phil Donahue, and was more than happy to build her an adjacent nursery for Parker.

Rosie knew of course that doing a talk show was a risk. Plenty of them had failed in recent years, and for a major entertainment figure, such a failure could be extremely damaging, as it had been for Chevy Chase. On the other hand, she was buoyed by the rapidity with which stations across the country picked up her show for syndication. Before it even went on the air it had a 93 percent market penetration. There were doubters, though—station executives who took note of the recent talk show casualty list, or who based their rejection on the fact that no actor had ever succeeded as a talk show host. Those who took the latter line simply hadn't been paying attention to Rosie's career. She was chiefly known as an actress at this point in her career, but she had gotten there through her stand-up work and cable television stints. And Rosie had started gaining experience as an emcee back in her late teens, at Long Island clubs. It was this early experience that counted most in being able to handle a talk show; her acting career had simply given her the name recognition to get people to tune in, as well as a wide acquaintance among the Hollywood performers who would be her guests.

Warner and Rosie were quick to agree on starting the show in June 1996, instead of waiting for the new fall season. There were a number of good reasons for taking this route. Because there were few start-up shows in the summer months, there wold be less competition for media and attention as well as viewers. The summer months would also give Rosie a tryout period to fine-tune the program before the fall season, when daytime viewership always increased in the aftermath of beach days and vacations. Also, some shows would be leaving the air in May, after long or curtailed runs, opening up programming slots at hundreds of television stations glad to have almost anything fresh to put on in place of shows that had sagged or bombed in the ratings.

With the logistics falling into place, Rosie began giving interviews to magazines and later, closer to the show's debut, on television shows. There was no problem lining up such interviews. It was known far and wide, thanks to her many promotional forays for her movies, that few celebrities were more quotable than Rosie or easier to deal with in an interview. One of the most interesting of the magazine interviews appeared in the June 1996 issue of *Allure,* which hit the stands about a month before her show went on the air. The article was written by Tom Shales, the often acerbic television critic for *The Washington Post.*

Tom Shales is known for being tough, and he did sound a few skeptical notes in his piece. He wrote of Rosie wading "into the wilds of Oprahland—the ferociously competitive arena of daytime TV," and reacted to her optimism with the comment "Of course, she's assuming things will go smoothly, which is always a mistake in television." He also granted that "her notion that the viewing public wants a daytime talk show without sleaze or sensationalism may not be as loopy as it sounds. In the past few months, tabloid talkers have been toppling like dominoes." He quoted Rosie herself sending up the urge to be sensationalistic: "Now watch. Come the first ratings period and we'll have 'Midget mass murderers—today on *Rosie!*' "

Shales clearly liked Rosie, commenting after her midget-mass-murder quote, "She says it self-effacingly, as she says most things." Although he quoted her at length about her problems with weight, he wrote, ". . . when she stands up and says good-bye to all the waiters, she doesn't look nearly as huge as she thinks she is. Besides, she has a tremendously cute face, and faces are what count on TV."

•   •   •

I hope the show's a hit, because then, in five years, you won't see me anymore. I've got a five-year deal. I'll do it for five years and go "Thanks for the money and good night." Then I'm going to work for child advocacy. When you have that much money, what the hell are you going to do with your life? If I was Oprah you'd never see me again. Ever.

Rosie O'Donnell to Tom Shales, in *Allure,* June 1996

•   •   •

With Shales, and in every other interview, Rosie emphasized what the show was *not* going to be. She told *Life:* "People shouldn't mistake it for a dysfunctional family show. It'll be a little monologue, a guest, maybe Susan Sarandon, a comedy piece, then, say, Garth Brooks to sing. I love his music. I'm much more middle-American than anybody ever realized." Rosie was not just reciting names from off the top of her head. Susan Sarandon had just won the Best Actress Oscar for *Dead Man Walking,* and Garth Brooks was one of the most popular singers in America. She would indeed get both of them on the show. To *Entertainment Weekly*, Rosie touted the fact that popular funnyman Martin Short would be on the show, as well as Nathan Lane, the Broadway comic genius who was having his first movie hit in *The Birdcage* with Robin Williams. She also told *Entertainment Weekly*, however, that she would "love to get Fergie. I think we'd just dish." This reference to the controversial Duchess of York, whose every move was then being chronicled by both the British and American tabloid press, was calculated to add a little spice to the mix. In this interview, Rosie also made it clear that she wouldn't be making any guests who were the object of tabloid slavering feel uncomfortable on her show. "I will not humiliate the guests and make them want to weep. Sure, if I get Lisa Marie, I'll want to know about Michael Jackson, but first I'll sit her down and say, 'How far do you want me to go?'"

With such statements, Rosie was accomplishing two objectives at once. She was letting potential viewers know that even though she would be doing a funny, friendly show, that didn't mean they wouldn't see some of the people whose names filled the gossip columns and supermarket tabloids. Pleasant and friendly, she was suggesting, didn't mean bland or dull. At the same time she was sending a signal to potential guests that they wouldn't have to worry about being ambushed on her show. If there was something they didn't want to get into, fine.

While many famous stars were slated for future shows, Rosie made the decision to start not with a huge bang but with guests who might appear on any average show over the coming months and, she hoped, years. As the show went out live to some East Coast markets (and was taped for the rest of the country) at 10:00 A.M. on Monday June 10, 1996, her first guest was George Clooney of the top-rated NBC drama *ER*. There was no question that Clooney was a star—his face had already appeared on a lot of magazine covers, and he was beginning to launch a movie career while continuing to do *ER*. On the other hand, he was not a mega star who had been a household name for years, like Bette Midler or Mel Gibson. In fact, Clooney, after presenting Rosie with a huge bouquet of roses, made a joke about his status, saying he was there only because Rosie's pal Madonna couldn't make it. Rosie told him that was right, setting up an extended joke that had him grabbing his roses back and smashing the bouquet over music director John McDaniel's piano.

Clooney was followed by the reigning queen of soap operas, Susan Lucci, famous not only for her bitchy Erica on *All My Children* but for having been nominated for a daytime Emmy every year for seventeen years without ever winning. Like Clooney, Lucci was a genuine name without being anything like a legend, except perhaps in the minds of her legions of soap fans. Rosie had followed *All My Children* quite faithfully over the years—one of the few soaps she had given that kind of attention to—and she thought Susan Lucci would be an entertaining guest that a great many daytime viewers would be happy to see. She was right.

Not only did Lucci's appearance go extremely well, but it led to Rosie making a guest appearance on *All My Children* in the role of a feisty maid at the end of July.

Clooney and Lucci set just the right tone for *The Rosie O'Donnell Show*. She had noted a mistake that she thought Joan Rivers had made with her show. "On her first show," Rosie said, "were Elton John, Cher, and all these people who were friends with her. And the next day, it was like she had the third lead from Bosom Buddies. I think you shoot yourself in the foot by doing that. My friends will come on when they have something to promote." Indeed, Penny Marshall, Tom Hanks, Madonna, Meg Ryan, and many other pals would later appear on the show. She would also ultimately snag not only Elton John, but also her two most desired guests, Tom Cruise and Barbra Streisand. Ultimately, almost everyone in show business would *want* to be on Rosie's show because they saw how well she treated her guests.

Before going on the air on June 10, Rosie had done five warm-ups with audiences, to work out the kinks, which were mostly technical. The one area in which Rosie got a reputation for being a stern taskmaster, and was not always too nice about it, was the technical end of the show. She had no patience with technical foul-ups, even though she had not made matters easy by insisting on having an advanced push-button audio system right by her desk, which allowed her to control the instantaneous playing of a recorded song by one of her guests, a snippet of dialogue, or a prerecorded funny comment on the proceedings. This was

a complicated setup, and one that the sound people sometimes seemed intent on sabotaging in the early run of the
show. While Rosie never stated it publicly, it was apparent
that the sound people were resisting her control over technical functions that they felt were their responsibility.

·   ·   ·

*You know when you go on a roller coaster and it clicks up
and then right after the last click before you go into the
whoosh? That's what I feel [when I go onstage]. It's almost
like when the audience member is doing the opening announcement, I hear the click and then I just go for the ride.
It's the one hour I don't have to think in the day. It's like
free time, like a kid in nursery school where you get a one
hour nap. The hour I'm there, I don't have to think of anything else. I just have to be in the moment.*

Rosie O'Donnell in *US,* October 1997

·   ·   ·

The glitches on opening day were minor, and the show
established from the start a fresh, funny, casual atmosphere
that was very different from the deliberately tension-filled
ambience that marked most daytime shows on the air, with
their sensational and controversial topics and agitated guests.
A number of recurring elements were put in place right at
the beginning. In a major—and original—departure from

customary practice, Rosie had an audience member give the introductory spiel that brought her onstage. Sometimes these individuals were people she knew well—from a former teacher to her own sister Maureen—sometimes they were set up in advance to showcase a charitable event or topic Rosie wanted to talk about, but on the first show, and most often after that, the person was an unknown selected from the studio audience. This novel idea served two purposes. First, it gave Rosie something spontaneous to react to at the beginning of the show each day as she chatted briefly and humorously with that day's chosen announcer. Second, in a larger and perhaps even more important sense, it gave the studio audience, and through it the viewer at home, the feeling of being a participant and not just a passive onlooker.

Other aspects of the show enhanced that feeling from the first day on. Every audience member was given a snack and a drink—originally Rosie's beloved Drakes cakes and low-fat milk, with other goodies introduced later on. After her initial casual remarks, which were not a formal monologue in *Tonight Show* tradition but contained a number of laugh lines, made standing at the front of the stage, Rosie would take her place at her desk and chat with bandleader John McDaniel, who had been the musical director for *Grease*. Friendly but low-key, given to a chuckle or giggle rather than an Ed MacMahon–type hearty laugh, McDaniel radiates a feeling of being part of Rosie's family, and their conversation, usually focused on a movie or show seen the night before, tends to sound overheard rather than set up. This too enhances the aura of informal friendliness, the feeling that the viewer has dropped in on a coffee klatch. Even Regis Philbin and Kathie Lee Gifford seem programmed and a mite pretentious when compared with Rosie's show.

On the first show, Rosie picked up a newspaper after her chat with McDaniel, and letting the audience in on the fact that there was a joke taped to each page, proceeded to do a bit of stand-up sitting down. This worked well, and Rosie continued to use it for some time, but eventually she moved on to several other ways of amusing the audience before her first guest was introduced. On the opening show, Rosie also started the routine of shooting Koosh balls—brightly colored round sponges—into the audience with a slingshot whenever the urge struck. For audience members, of course, these became treasured souvenirs.

When the Nielsen ratings came in, *The Rosie O'Donnell Show* had scored a 3.2 rating for the first program (a ratings point represents 960,000 homes tuned in). These were the highest debut numbers for a syndicated program since *The Oprah Winfrey Show* a decade earlier. And they weren't just a onetime "let's check this out" high. They held steady for the first two weeks, and then began to climb higher, moving up to a 3.9 rating by the middle of the following month. In the high-stakes New York area market, the number of viewers was almost double the national average of her debut show, hitting a 6.0, a full ratings point higher than *Live with Regis and Kathie Lee*.

There had always been some movie reviewers who didn't "get" Rosie O'Donnell, perhaps most famously the powerful Roger Ebert, who had said of her in *Exit to Eden*, "I've seen her in three or four movies now, and she has generally had the same effect on me as fingernails on a blackboard." But almost all the television critics seemed to grasp what she was after with her new talk show, and they gave her very high marks for achievement. There's a big difference between the national readership of *People* and the very New York readership of *The Village Voice,* but both publications thought she was a refreshing change, with the first praising her "realness" and "authenticity," and the second her ability to be "sassy without being mean."

The showbiz-oriented publications were on board, too. Weekly *Variety*'s Todd Everett noted that "her most striking feature may be her seeming accessibility; she seems closer to the audience than any other host in memory." *Entertainment Weekly* said that she delivered "a refreshing dose of spunk, fire, and genuine fun." And the often sour Jeff Jarvis of *TV Guide* went on at length about how she was bringing fun to television, touting her over David Letterman, Jay Leno, and Kathie Lee Gifford. He concluded, "She may just be the first person to take the night out of *Tonight.* And in the process, she's making daytime a nicer place."

Numerous critics took note of the rapport she established with her guests because of her real knowledge of show business. Todd Everett deemed Rosie "a far better interviewer than any of the late-night variety show hosts in recent memory; for one thing she seems to know who her guests are." *Time*'s Gina Bellafante noted that she didn't "exploit guests for her own comedy. She can talk to them rather than at them because she actually goes to the movies and watches

TV." In *USA Today*, Matt Roush similarly declared, "Rosie's greatest strength may be her unembarrassed love for TV. She knows whereof she watches."

Rosie's knowledge of television shows of the late 1960s on was almost awe-inspiring. *The Partridge Family, Eight Is Enough, The Brady Bunch,* and her favorite, *The Mary Tyler Moore Show,* were series whose every episode, it sometimes seemed, she knew by heart. She was able to astonish guests like Florence Henderson of *The Brady Bunch* with her memory for arcane details. "Remember when . . . ," Rosie would begin, and soon the guest's jaw would be dropping. It was the same for Broadway shows, movies, and pop singers' albums. Her clear delight in meeting the favorite actors and singers of her childhood naturally charmed her guests. But once, early on, there was a very bad moment.

On most talk shows and interview programs, it is the guests who sometimes find themselves in shock because the host has asked a rude, prying, personal question, occasionally even one that the host has promised not to ask. That kind of situation can backfire on the interviewer. But Rosie had made it clear ahead of time that she wasn't going to do that kind of thing to her guests, and because she proved as good as her word, there are few shows, if any, that celebrities are happier to appear on.

However, in the first week of *The Rosie O'Donnell Show,* there was an incident that eventually made it necessary for the guest to apologize to her—an unusual turnaround. The culprit was Donny Osmond. Rosie had been a fan of his back in the days when he and his sister Marie were topping the record charts, and she was looking forward to his appearance. She even showed off a Donny Osmond lunch pail and doll, brought out from her bottomless collection of pop memorabilia. At one point, Osmond started talking about an appearance he was to make at Brigham Young University on the Fourth of July, which would involved his making an entrance dangling from a helicopter. Rosie jokingly offered to serve as his stunt person because "I don't want you to get hurt." Osmond replied that it was going to be fun, and added, ". . . the helicopter can't handle that much weight."

Nine months later, Oprah Winfrey interviewed Rosie on her show and brought up the incident in the context of people's insensitivity about weight; Rosie recalled her feeling shocked at the time and thinking, "Did he just make a fat joke about me?" Winfrey said, "I was watching that day." "But then you have to see the tape, because the look on my face is like, yeah . . . I think . . . once I realized—it registered—he did indeed make a fat joke; now attack him. So I had to, you know."

Rosie didn't go after him then and there. But she brought it up on her next show, and then again, and for a time it became a running joke, that always had the audience squarely on Rosie's side. Then the media took it up, and Donny Osmond found himself getting slammed from every direction. He sent Rosie flowers and insisted he'd just been kidding, but the press was still after him, and almost six weeks later he returned to the show to apologize in person on the air. Rosie didn't make it easy for him, enlisting his sister Marie to come on and tell stories about how Donny had teased her. Rosie would tell Oprah Winfrey that when she got in touch with Marie to ask her if she'd help give her brother a hard time, Marie replied, "Yes, in a heartbeat." That was only part of Rosie's revenge. As Oprah noted, "Oh, the best though, was the puppy suit when he came back. That was the best."

Indeed, the puppy suit proved a highlight of the early shows. She handed him the costume and told him he had to put it on and sing his old song "Puppy Love" to her on bended knee. "He had no idea we were going to do the puppy suit," Rosie told Oprah. Osmond had little choice but to humiliate himself, and Rosie not only forgave him on air but would later note that he'd been a very good sport about it. But the incident never really died: Paul Anka, who had originally recorded "Puppy Love," came on the show and insisted on singing it to Rosie as it ought to be performed, to the delight of both Rosie and the audience. Even months later, one guest or another would bring up the "Donny Osmond incident," giving Rosie a chance to roll her eyes and deliver a new laugh line. Poor Donny Osmond had no idea what he was letting himself in for when he tangled with Rosie.

Of course, the Osmond controversy only helped Rosie's show. It certainly didn't damage her reputation as someone with an idea so old—be nice to your guests—that it seemed new all over again. In fact, within two weeks, Rosie was on the cover of *Newsweek,* wearing a bright red jacket, a white shirt, and a striped vest, sporting a big smile, with the words QUEEN OF NICE emblazoned across her chest in huge letters. A smaller headline asked the question, CAN ROSIE O'DONNELL CLEAN UP TRASH TV? The fingers of Rosie's upraised hands were crossed in answer to that one. As she told viewers, she would look at the cover on the newsstands and wonder for half a minute who that was before realizing, "Oh, yeah, that's me." The article inside *Newsweek* was as much about television in general and the decline of manners in our society in particular as it was about Rosie herself. Soon, however, it seemed that every magazine on the market had Rosie on the cover and contained an article focused entirely on her life, humor, and wisdom.

. . .

I've been demoted to Princess of Nice, by the way. . . . I don't know; I never wanted to be mean, and I don't think it's funny to be mean. I don't want to make a joke about somebody and then walk into a party and see them, and feel embarrassed that I possibly hurt their feelings. I know the writers get frustrated by that sometimes.

Rosie O'Donnell in a dialogue with her head writer, Randy Cohen,
in *Entertainment Weekly,* 1995

. . .

Television stations around the country began putting her show into better time slots to capitalize on her popularity. It seemed there was no one in show business who didn't want to be on her show. Cher, Bette Midler, and Roseanne Barr, the three "dream" guests shown with Rosie in that cartoon in *Glamour* magazine, all showed up in due course. Of course, there were a couple of holdouts going by the names of Tom Cruise and Barbra Streisand. But did anyone really think they could resist forever?

NINE

Self-image and Public Image

In a society that at times seems to prize thinness more than anything except money, Rosie O'Donnell has always been at an apparent disadvantage. But her weight has not always worked against her, and although she has often talked about it, she has never seemed obsessed about it the way many women are. As she told Liz Smith in a *Good Housekeeping* interview, "I try to be healthy, but the fact is I usually don't succeed with diets. I will never go on one of these big diet regimens. You're supposed to try to be happy with who you are. When Penny Marshall cast me in *A League of Their Own,* she said, 'I want you to lose twenty pounds.' And I said, 'Penny, if I *could* lose twenty pounds, I *would.* I don't walk around going, 'I like to be a little overweight.' People say to me, 'Well, now you have money, why don't you hire a cook?' It's like, if you have money, you should be thin. As though success solves all your mental problems."

. . .

It's my constant struggle. The very sad thing about my weight is when I'm thin—like when I did <u>Grease</u> on Broadway and was working out every day and got down to a 32-inch jean, which for me is very small—I never appreciate it. I can be 150 or 180 and I don't feel any different. When I look in the mirror, I still see myself as heavy, even if I get thinner. I never enjoy it even when I'm at the lower weight . . . the way I carry my weight is like a big old beer-guzzling man. I have a huge stomach. I don't have a big-girl butt, I have a big tummy and it's really bad.

Rosie O'Donnell to Liz Smith, in *Good Housekeeping,* June 1997

. . .

Depending on what kinds of questions are asked about her weight, or sometimes perhaps just according to her mood, Rosie takes several tacks in discussing the issue. She has noted many times that her mother was stocky, and that Irish women often tend to be slightly on the heavy side. Sometimes she abandons this genetic approach in favor of a psychological one. In an interview with Hollywood reporter Chantal on *Good Morning America* in 1994, Rosie said, ". . . if it was simply about food, nobody would be overweight. It's about all the emotions connected to it, and why you do it, and why you need to disguise yourself to feel safer . . . I mean, it's years and years of therapy, and it's a lifelong struggle, and not necessarily to be thin, but to be at a place where you can, you know, feel your own body and yourself connected to your body."

In the same interview, Rosie carried this idea back to its source in her own life. "And I noticed before my mother died, the pictures of my family, we were all fairly normal sized. And then a year after, there were some pictures, and we were all big. We were all, you know, trying to satiate ourselves, in ways that were no longer nurtured, through food."

There have been times when Rosie has lost weight, and got down to what is thin for her, about 150 pounds and a 32-inch waist. She did that for *Exit to Eden,* which required her to wear skimpy erotic costumes. Magazines were more than happy to feature publicity stills showing her in these getups. Her weight was down similarly for her Broadway run in *Grease,* which was partly a matter of determination, and partly a result of the physical exertion involved in an eight-performance-a-week schedule in a show that called for a lot of movement and dancing.

Rosie has also indicated that being thinner doesn't give her all that much satisfaction, that she doesn't *enjoy* being thin enough to stay that way. Her consciousness of her own weight is largely determined by the clothes she can wear at a given time—which is a way of declaring that she refuses to be chained to a scale. She also seems aware that being somewhat heavy allows many people to relate to her more fully "because they can see me, too, struggle publicly with it." There are more than enough thin women on television, and it's likely that many of her fans are happy to see someone who isn't thin, and doesn't appear to be desperate about it, on television five days a week. It adds to Rosie's down-home image, and seems a part of the "comfort factor" that endears her to many viewers. She has noted, humorously, that fans who encounter her in the flesh often say, "God, I thought you'd be *fatta*." To which Rosie's attitude is "Oh, thank you, that's sweet."

As she was gearing up to do her show, Rosie told television critic Tom Shales, "I'm going to try not to discuss it on the show, not to do jokes about my weight. I don't want little kids who are overweight to think that looking like me is bad." This was not a resolution Rosie was able to keep. Perhaps because she heard too many people say in the early part of her career that she was "too tough, too heavy," there is a degree of bravado involved in flaunting her weight. It's a way of saying, "What do you know?" Or perhaps it's because she has used her weight to be funny for so long that it is an integral part of her act. It is also clear that Rosie simply loves food, and loves to talk about it—and her obvious pleasure in eating takes a lot of the sting out of any jokes she may make about being overweight. At the end of her appearance on *The View* in November 1997 with Barbara Walters, Rosie was confronted with a coffeetable full of edible goodies prepared by another guest, her pal Naomi Judd. Judd urged her to try a sausage ball, to which Rosie replied,

"Naomi, you give me a choice between a cookie, a brownie, and a sausage ball, it's not going to be the sausage ball, trust me." As with so much of what Rosie says, there is something wonderfully real about this remark. You can almost hear people at home chuckling because that is exactly what they would say.

. . .

It's hard to meet people. I'm dating a guy now, he's on TV. You might know him. He's on America's Most Wanted. You know, Sally, he looks a lot better than that sketch. He really does. I'm telling you right now. Whenever he gets out of line . . . I go, 'Hey, I've got that 1-800 number, buddy.'

Rosie O'Donnell to Sally Jessy Raphaël, July 1990

. . .

Rosie has been forthcoming about her crushes on male movie stars, such as heartthrob Tom Cruise. In the fall of 1996, Rosie began a major campaign to get Cruise to appear on her show. Punching up "Tommy Can You Hear Me?" from the rock opera *Tommy* at the slightest excuse on her audio machine by her desk, Rosie made her courtship of Cruise a running joke for weeks on end. The audience loved it and Rosie played it for all it was worth (and then some, a minority complained).

As she subsequently told Liz Smith, Rosie had "always loved him. I don't know how to explain it. It's like a chemical reaction; it's totally a teenage, prepubescent-girl crush. I don't want to marry the man; I don't want to be naked in bed with him. I just want him to walk around my yard— maybe, you know, with a rake or a hoe. I just find him to be like an old-time movie star, like Clark Gable. He's dashing, intelligent, funny, and sexy."

Cruise upped the ante himself by sending her a note and flowers. Rosie then got to meet him in person when she was asked to emcee the annual Moving Picture Ball put on by the American Cinemateque. Flying to Los Angeles for the September 21 bash, Rosie had a fake tattoo placed just above her left breast that read "Tom." This was appropriate, since Cruise was the year's honoree, and Rosie got a major laugh and much applause when she suddenly tugged down the top of her dress to display it. Back in New York, he called her while her show was in progress to thank her for emceeing the event.

Cruise subsequently agreed to appear on Rosie's show on December 10, when he would be promoting his new movie *Jerry Maguire,* which would become a major hit and garner him his second Oscar nomination as Best Actor. A countdown to the big day was inaugurated on the show, with Rosie finding a way to make endless jokes about her obsession with him. The day before his appearance, she had his wife, Nicole Kidman, come on the show to play out her role as "jealous wife" to much audience delight. Tom's actual appearance, which might well have proved a letdown after all the buildup, went extremely well, with Cruise—one of the better interview subjects in Hollywood—clearly less nervous than Rosie. They concluded the show by having their pictures taken together in an old-fashioned instant photo booth that Rosie had installed onstage. The show received the highest rating yet, as even more casual daytime viewers tuned in for the big event.

• • •

[The day Tom Cruise was on] was probably my favorite show so far. But it was also the one where I was most nervous. When you have a crush on somebody, it almost ruins it to meet them. I was worried that he'd think I was insane, since I profess my love for him to millions of people on a daily basis. I was worried that he'd think I was wacko. But he was such a great sport. He kidded around with me.

Rosie O'Donnell to Liz Smith, 1997

• • •

Another theme of Rosie's show has been her love of children—not just her own son, Parker, but all children. Her show segment featuring jokes and cartoons sent in by kids proved very popular, and the book she compiled from it, *Kids Are Punny,* became a major paperback best-seller. The money from the book went to Rosie's own For All Kids Foundation, as would $10 from the sale of each of the Rosie dolls introduced in November 1997. She also raised nearly $500,000 for her own and other charitable organizations by parlaying an insult into a fund-raising bonanza. The mouthwash Scope had put out an ad saying that according to a survey, Rosie had been deemed, along with Tom Brokaow of NBC News and others, as being one of the "least kissable people" on television. Rosie made an arrangement with the rival mouthwash Listerine that every time a guest kissed her on the show, the company would donate $100 to charity. An electronic tally was flashed on the screen for each kiss, and the amount escalated by several hundred dollars a day. Listerine sales shot up, charity was served, and the makers of Scope were left blue in the face.

Rosie, who had broken with talk show tradition by declaring herself a firm Democrat, discussed children's issues on air with no less than Hillary Clinton and Tipper Gore. In one of her few nods to the darker side of television talk shows, she excoriated Woody Allen for his affair with Mia Farro's adopted daughter while praising Farrow to the skies (her only other really nasty comments were reserved for O. J. Simpson).

When she was labeled "The Queen of Nice" by *Newsweek* after her show had only been on the air two weeks, she had worried about living up to the designation, protesting that she wasn't all that nice. Plus the tabloids quickly tried to deflate the "nice" image by reporting on backstage discord at the show. But the public heard that kind of story about *every* television show. As she told Mim Udovitch in *US,* "I think a director and the producer and star of a show, which is what I am, have a sort of marriage. So we kind of dated a few people, and now we're trying to get married." That issue, too, soon dissipated.

The public seemed to think it was just fine that Rosie was making so much money from her show, too. She repeatedly emphasized that there was a point beyond which money became meaningless, and that eventually she expected to devote herself to charitable work and children's issues. Her purchase of the late Helen Hayes's estate in Nyack, New York, was not seen as being an example of Beverly Hills–type conspicuous consumption. Hayes had for decades been regarded as one of America's greatest stage actresses (she had won a couple of Oscars, too, for Best Actress in the 1931 talkie *The Sin of Madelon Claudet,* and for Best Supporting Actress in 1970's *Airport*). Rosie told *Life,* "I was a huge fan of hers. The night she met [playwright and future husband] Charles MacArthur, he poured peanuts into her hands and said, 'I wish they were emeralds.' Years later, after they were really successful, he poured emeralds into her hands and said, 'I wish they were peanuts.' " This was the kind of well-known anecdote Rosie would like, one that underscored her mixture of romanticism and down-to-earth common sense.

In every way, Rosie seemed to be dealing with her success in a way that avoided pretentiousness, and that amalgamated the fan she had been when growing up and the star she had become. There she was on her own show, talking with one of her childhood idols, Bette Midler, one moment recalling how she had worshiped Bette and the next discussing their mutual experiences of motherhood. She could imitate her pal Cher on the show in a way that Cher wryly described as "a little too good." She could joke about everyone in America having seen her close friend Madonna's breasts, or say, referring to the father of Madonna's child, "She sleeps with her trainer, I ignore mine."

As Mim Udovitch noted, "To watch her greet John Travolta with a gesture that's half shaking hands with a peer and half dancing starstruck at a cousin's wedding is to see the wishes of the audience made real in a tangible way, a way that anyone could imagine being a part of."

People believed Rosie when she said that it always took a moment to adjust to seeing herself on a magazine cover. For once, it made sense when a star talked about the burdens of fame—because she wasn't worried about herself but about the problems it would create for her children. She did have one complaint about her fans, though. "I'll say, 'Hi, I'm Rosie.' And people are like, 'I know.' As if I'm not supposed to introduce myself. As if I should just say, 'Nice to meet you, you know me.'" Such a Rosie kind of complaint. Funny, and endearing and real. With Rosie, as with so few famous people, what you saw was what you got. The real person and the public image were one and the same.

A Tony Experience

TEN

The announcement in the first week of May 1997 that the annual Broadway Tony Awards show was to be hosted by Rosie O'Donnell was not met with universal enthusiasm within the theater community. Not that anyone went on the record with their objections, but *The New York Times* weekly theater news column, the gossip columnists for the *Daily News* and the *New York Post,* as well as the show business bible *Variety,* all reported anonymous grumblings from some of Broadway's old guard. While it was true that Rosie had been the star of the 1994 revival of *Grease,* she was nevertheless regarded as primarily a creature of television and the movies, not the theater. There had been objections in the past when CBS, in an attempt to boost the ratings for these least-watched of the major show business award shows, had stocked the list of Tony presenters with too many television stars who had not appeared on Broadway for years. And that was just presenters, not the host for the entire evening. What's more, Rosie had never even been nominated for a Tony Award, much less won one. As far as some members of the theater community were concerned, the ideal host had been Angela Lansbury, who had presided over the festivities for three years in the early 1990s. She had been chosen by CBS because she was one of their biggest television stars, having anchored their Sunday night lineup for years as Jessica Fletcher on *Murder, She Wrote.* Angela had also won four Tony Awards as Best Actress in a Musical—for *Mame* (1966), *Dear World* (1969), her revival of *Gypsy* (1975), and *Sweeney Todd* (1979), more than any other musical actress had received. She was a theater legend long before she was a television star.

Quite aside from Rosie's thin claims to theatrical legitimacy, some theater people were aghast at the locale for the presentation of the Fifty-first Tony Awards, Radio City Music Hall, which had been Rosie's suggestion. To some producers, it was reported, this was seen as heresy; the awards had never before been broadcast from anything but a legitimate Broadway theater. Radio City might be a grand hall, but it was a movie palace! What's more, they were going to *sell* tickets in order to fill its vast auditorium. Never mind that there were lots of people thrilled at the opportunity to buy a ticket to a Tony Awards show, and that from that standpoint the idea was terrific public relations. Broadway's old guard liked the fact that the Tony Awards had always been an exclusive event that even many theater people couldn't get into. It didn't seem to occur to them that such exclusivity and elitism might be one reason why the Tony Awards were not a bigger draw on television.

The one idea that Rosie had come up with that gained approval was to split the broadcast of the show between CBS and the Public Broadcasting System, with an hour on PBS followed by two hours on the commercial network. This arrangement would take care of a major problem. For years, the Tonys had been a three-hour broadcast; recently, however, the program had not only been squeezed into two hours, but there had been an ironclad rule that it could not run over that time period and had to end promptly at 11:00 P.M., so that the affiliate stations across the country didn't have to delay their local news roundups. The actual presentation in New York had continued to run for a full three hours, but the winners in the technical categories like Sets, Costumes, and Lighting were shown in abbreviated clips that cut their acceptance speeches out; or, worse, their names had been read off during the broadcast by some star onstage while the winners stood up for ten seconds at their seats in the audience, like kids at a high school assembly. The PBS broadcast would mean that for those who were interested across the country, these artists would get their full moment in the spotlight.

Thus on Sunday night, June 1, 1996, the PBS segment began at 8:00 P.M. with shots of the full audience in attendance at Radio City Music Hall. Then there was a brief introduction from Rosie herself, informally dressed in a white open-necked top, welcoming viewers to a program covering every aspect of a Broadway production from sets to choreography. She told the audience that she had to go get changed into her "dress," which would prove to be a black pantssuit with a sequined top, and that she'd see everybody later on CBS. The hour that followed turned out to be both informative and entertaining in the best PBS tradition, with interviews of all the nominees in the design and other creative categories, numerous backstage clips of rehearsals and set construction, and a true inside look at the theater business. The awards were given out at Radio City in the categories of Sets, Costumes, Lighting, Book and Score of a Musical, Orchestration, Choreography, Director of a Play and of a Musical. Nor was there any shortage of stars to hand out these awards, with presentations made by such famous Tony winners as Chita Rivera, Joel Grey, Liza Minnelli, Hal Holbrook, and Lauren Bacall.

At nine o'clock, the action switched to CBS. With the announcement of "Our host for the evening, Rosie O'Donnell," Rosie made her entrance through a door erected at center stage and immediately launched into a specialty song, "On Broadway," which she delivered with panache and far better control of the notes than sometimes heard in her impromptu renditions of songs on her program. She had rehearsed hard for this night, and it showed. She was soon joined by two tuxedo-clad male dancers, which gave her a chance to show off a vintage Rosie routine as she expressed displeasure at their presence by announcing, "This is a solo," drawing a big laugh from the audience. She also kidded her own singing ability in the lyrics, warbling, "Remember me,

I used to be, On Broadway, I twirled a hula hoop, I sang off key . . ."

• • •

I actually wanted to be a Broadway actress because I grew up here in New York, on Long Island, and I used to come to the city and see Broadway shows with my mom when I was a little girl. And that was my only sort of relationship with real live people who did this thing for a living. I'd see movies, but I'd never met them. I didn't know where they lived, who they were—but I'd come to see a Broadway show, I'd stand outside the stage door, and I saw the people who had just done the show. So that was really my first love . . . to be a Broadway star.

Rosie O'Donnell to Al Roker of CNBC, April 1995

• • •

The number then opened up with the casts of every musical from previous years still running on Broadway singing signature numbers from their shows, and Rosie joining in. Starting with the previous year's Best Musical, *Rent,* and including the champion of all musicals in terms of durability, *Cats,* one show after another was showcased, including a sequence from *Smokey Joe's Cafe* that gave Rosie a chance to show off her footwork as she joined the women of the cast in singing and dancing "I'm a Woman." The opening number achieved a special excitement as Rosie was joined by ten men in black leather jackets from her own still-running Broadway show, *Grease.* They sang a restaged-for-the-Tonys version of "Greased Lightning," sung in the actual show by Kenickie, not Rizzo, whom Rosie had played. She brought this number off with great zest, and the seven-and-a-half-minute opening number then closed with musical repartee between Rosie and the cast of singing crockery from *Sleeping Beauty.*

Rosie said later that rehearsals for this long sequence had been time-consuming and arduous, but all the hard work certainly paid off on Tony night. The audience reaction was extremely enthusiastic, the great range of musical experiences available to Broadway theatergoers was displayed to viewers across the country, and the results kept up the Tony tradition of doing an opening number vastly superior to those usually seen on the Oscars and other award shows. Rosie herself had seemed at ease, in command, and was clearly having a wonderful time. While she herself had said many times that she was hardly in the same category as the usual Broadway musical luminary, she showed conclusively that she could bring off a number designed around her, as this one had been, with style and professionalism. While her fans at home were probably unsurprised at her success, it seems likely that some in the live audience who had been unhappy with her being chosen as host may have begun to be won over with this display of theatrical pizzazz.

After a commercial break, Rosie reappeared to welcome

viewers to "a special night for Broadway and a special night for me." She then got a big laugh by informing the audience that she had sung the entire score of *Les Misérables* during the PBS portion of the show, and that though "I don't meant to boast, I'm a phenomenal Jean Valjean." She got another big laugh by warning that if any of the winners talked too long, "they simply lower the stage and let them meet the camels from the Nativity scene that live downstairs." This remark was funny, not only as a reminder of past Tony time shortages, but served as a good-natured tweak of those unhappy with Radio City Music Hall as the evening's venue. It was clear to many in the Tony audience, as subsequent comments would reveal, that she would be happy to send the complainers down to meet the camels.

After this introduction, however, Rosie kept the jokes to a minimum while she was on the air, although it was reported afterward that she kept the Radio City Musical Hall audience in stitches with a steady stream of funny remarks during the commercial breaks. This in itself was unusual—the Tony host usually disappeared entirely from view during commercials. But Rosie, as she had during her movie career from *A League of Their Own* onward, saw it as her duty to keep the troops amused during "downtime."

Rosie announced each actor or actress who came onstage to hand out an award with effusive comments about their talent and her own admiration for them. Of Roseanne Barr, her fellow stand-up comedian, who was in New York to play the Wicked Witch of the West in *The Wizard of Oz,* Rosie said, "When it comes to comedy, the lady is nothing less than a national treasure." The elegantly dressed Roseanne then proceeded to entertain the Tony audience with a series of nonraunchy jokes entirely suited to the occasion. Later, Rosie announced, "As her biggest fan it is an incredible thrill to be able for me to introduce to you the lady I want to be when I grow up, Miss Julie Andrews." And she even sang her introduction of Tony and Emmy winner Mandy Patinkin.

Among the other presenters were Dixie Carter, who was on Broadway playing Maria Callas in the long-running play *Master Class,* Whoopi Goldberg, who had taken over the lead in *A Funny Thing Happened on the Way to the Forum* from Tony winner Nathan Lane, Alec Baldwin, a previous Tony nominee for a revival of *A Streetcar Named Desire,* long-time theater stalwart Rip Torn, two-time supporting actress Tony winner Christine Baranski, who had recently won an Emmy for her tippling sophisticate on TV's *Cybil,* and the previous year's Best Actress Oscar winner Susan Sarandon, whom Rosie had seen onstage in 1982 in *Extremities* in a performance she termed "simply amazing." Sarandon had been personally recruited for the Tony show by Rosie, as had her beloved Mary Tyler Moore.

It had also been Rosie's idea that each presenter begin by recalling how he or she had been attracted to the theater in the first place. This resulted in far more engaging remarks than were usually the case on any award show, as memories that were sometimes touching and sometimes funny were related by the stars. Top honors in the humor category went to Roseanne, who noted that she had grown up in Salt Lake

City, Utah, and that while Mormons were "very entertaining," she had known there "must be more," and to Susan Sarandon, who recounted that her first theater experience had been to see Mary Martin in *Peter Pan*, from which she had learned that "fairies can always be revived by applause," a line that was much appreciated by the audience.

Rosie broke with tradition by clearly indicating which of the nominated musicals was her personal favorite. After the excerpt from *Titanic* was performed, she said, "Sail on *Titanic*. I love that show." She had been boosting the show since she first saw it in previews, even after it opened to mixed reviews. Earlier in the evening, on the PBS broadcast, the show had won the Tonys for Best Book, Best Score, Best Sets, and Best Orchestration, suggesting that it was likely to win the Best Musical award as well, so Rosie was on fairly safe ground in making her admiration for it known, but it was a departure for the host to do any rooting for a show. *Titanic* did indeed win the Tony for Best Musical and went on to become the hottest ticket on Broadway, bringing to a triumphant conclusion the saga of this most expensive (at $10 million) Broadway production ever.

At the end of the show, Rosie announced with pride, "We came in right on time," and closed by saying, "I humbly thank all of you for allowing me to be here." By the next day, the thanks were flowing in the other direction. With Rosie at the helm and the change to the Radio City Music Hall venue, the long run of low ratings for the Tony telecast was stunningly reversed. Weekly *Variety* headed its account of this comeback KUDOCAST BASKS IN ROSIE GLOW. The *Va-*

riety story opened, "Just when it looked as if the Tony Awards had degenerated into a ratings albatross around the neck of CBS, the June 1 telecast of the 51st Tonys rode the crest of Rosie O'Donnell's swelling popularity to the broadcast's highest ratings in a decade." It went on to note that ". . . this year's show gave CBS a 9.6 rating/16 share in the Nielsen nationals—a nifty 48 percent improvement on the 1996 household figures and a phenomenal 81 percent above that year's rating with adults 25 to 54."

Rosie's triumph was heightened by the fact that the telecast had been aired opposite the first game of the NBA Finals on NBC. These figures were of great significance to Broadway producers. Not only did they mean much greater exposure of Broadway's offerings to a national audience, which could only result in increased ticket sales down the line, but the numbers also seemed likely to salvage the commercial broadcast of the Tony Awards for the future. CBS had been broadcasting the awards since 1978, but this was the final show under the current contract, and in the previous year there had been much doubt in theater circles that the network would pick up its option for renewal. That had led to speculation that the entire show might have to be broadcast on PBS or even cable in the future, with correspondingly lower viewership. Now it seemed likely that CBS would pick up its option—as it subsequently announced it would do.

The majority of the credit for this turnaround went directly to Rosie herself. She had tirelessly plugged the awards telecast on her show, and spent an entire week showcasing the season's new musicals. Her own longstanding love of Broadway, reiterated again and again, had clearly proved infectious. The addition of the early PBS hour, the use of Radio City Music Hall, and her ability to pull in glamorous presenters had all proved to be major pluses. And credit was openly given. At the end of the Tony show, after the credits for the CBS producers and the director, the first of a long list of additional credits read: "Creative Consultant: Rosie O'Donnell." This was the first time such a credit had been given to the show's host, and it was obviously richly deserved. *The New York Times* reported that those who had been complaining beforehand about Rosie serving as host and about the shift to Radio City were completely silent in the aftermath of the Tonys. Far more than had been the case even when she headed the cast of *Grease* three years earlier, the bubbling Broadway fan from Commack, Long Island, was now being toasted by the most powerful people in the world of theater. The fan had shown the professionals how to salute their own and get the country to tune in to the festivities. The theater professionals, to show that they knew what had happened and express their gratitude, took out a full-page ad in the June 9–15 *Variety* picturing Rosie in her Tony duds, holding two Tony awards, with one of her patented "hey, gee" looks on her face. Across the top of the huge photo was emblazoned ROSIE, THANK YOU, and at the bottom, LOVE, THE AMERICAN THEATER WING AND THE LEAGUE OF AMERICAN THEATERS AND PRODUCERS.

There was no question now that the girl from Commack had conquered Broadway, and then some.

ELEVEN

Another Season,
Another Child

*T*he Rosie O'Donnell Show had had the most successful first season of any syndicated talk show since Oprah
Winfrey had gone national a decade earlier. Oprah had had
time to hone her skills and the shape of her show in Chicago
on a local basis before she took on the pressures of national
syndication. Rosie had started off with only a one-week
warmup run. True, Rosie was better known across the country when she started than Oprah had been, although Oprah
had received much attention for her role in Steven Spielberg's movie *The Color Purple,* and had been nominated for
an Oscar as Best Supporting Actress for 1985. But if Rosie
had not had as much experience hosting a talk show, she
had had a great deal of experience that fed into the talk show
format, especially her many years in stand-up comedy. Most
important, though, she had had exactly the right idea for
the kind of show that would fare well in the mid-1990s,

just as Oprah had sensed where the wind was blowing a decade earlier.

The press had tried to create the semblance of a bitter rivalry between the two women, which had no basis in truth but which circumstance had appeared to support at the time. When Rosie's close friend Madonna had appeared on Oprah's show to promote her lavish new musical film *Evita,* the gossips in the press, particularly the tabloids, were quick to suggest that Rosie was angry with Oprah and furious with Madonna. Some people seemed to believe all this at the time, even though Oprah, during her interview with Madonna, said she was "really disturbed" by the reports that she and Rosie hated one another. "I love Rosie," she said. "I watched Tom Cruise on Rosie myself the other day." Rosie said that she watched Oprah regularly and that Madonna had appeared on Oprah's show first because of scheduling, and would appear on Rosie's show in January 1997, which indeed she did.

Nevertheless, this was a topic that the two women still felt it necessary to deal with when Rosie herself appeared on *The Oprah Winfrey Show* on May 20, 1997. This was a particularly good time to try to set the record straight, since both women's shows had been nominated for the Daytime Emmy Award in the Talk Show category, and both were up against one another in the Talk Show Host category as well. Oprah welcomed Rosie by saying, "When Rosie said on her show that she wanted to be on my show, I have to tell you this. My people didn't want her to do it, and her people didn't want her to do it. Both sides said, 'No! You're competition! How could you?' Well, I'm thrilled that Rosie's here! Rosie's here!"

Rosie noted that the objections on her side of the fence were corporate ones. "Because, you know, there are two ways to think of yourself when you become an entertainer that earns a lot of money for a company . . . and one is as a person, which I hope I try to maintain my whole life, and the other as a corporate entity. So they're looking at me as a corporate entity." Both women agreed that retaining one's humanity was the important thing, but the corporate people did in fact have a point. For the week that Rosie appeared on Oprah's show, hers was the second most-watched daytime talk show on the air, as it had been all year, with only Oprah ahead of her. But there was a considerable gap between them. The list for syndicated shows that week, as reported in *Variety*, put *Wheel of Fortune* in first place, with a 10.8 rating, followed by *Jeopardy*, reruns of *Home Improvement*, and then *The Oprah Winfrey Show*, with a 7.8 rating. The next talk show on the list was *The Rosie O'Donnell Show*, with a 4.8 rating, just ahead of *Live with Regis and Kathie Lee*. But Rosie's show was in thirteenth place.

That would make it seem that Oprah had nothing to worry about, but in some major television markets, stations had moved Rosie's show directly opposite Oprah's, using it as a lead-in to the all-important local news. And in some locales, Rosie was beating Oprah, even if only by a slim margin. Rosie's corporate people naturally wanted her to beat Oprah in more markets, and Oprah's people didn't like what was happening in some markets at all. From that point of view, then, there was an edgy sense of competition, but the two women wanted nothing to do with it on a personal basis. They took rather sharp note of the fact that no one tried to manufacture such stories about nasty rivalries between men with competing shows. (They were forgetting about David Letterman and Jay Leno, but in general their point was well taken.)

Rosie was on Oprah's show for the full hour that day, and they discussed many people, including Madonna, Tom Cruise, and Mary Tyler Moore, and a wide range of topics, from weight to kids. In the course of things, Oprah brought up the fact that the Daytime Emmy Awards were to be handed out the next night, and said that she thought that Rosie would win and deserved to. Rosie was clearly touched. In fact, when the awards were handed out on May 21, the voters saw fit to divide the awards between them, making Oprah a winner in the Talk Show category and Rosie the winner as Talk Show Host. In one sense, Rosie was the overall winner here. To receive an Emmy for one's first full year on television is a signal honor, given only to those who offer real quality and establish a high degree of immediate popularity. Many talented people never win one. The co-host of the awards show that night was a case in point: Susan Lucci, who had been a guest on Rosie's very first show, had been nominated for the seventeenth time without winning. Thus Rosie's Emmy was a true capstone to a remarkable first year.

Talk shows, of course, are broadcast year round, with only a few breaks for the host to take a vacation, which are usually filled with reruns. Thus small changes in a show may take place at any time of year, and Rosie had made a number of them already, introducing new segments like the one featuring jokes and cartoons sent in by kids, and then moving on to something else when a routine began to get tired. There were no plans to seriously revamp the show for the 1997–1998 season. Behind the scenes one change had already taken place that indicated the degree of Rosie's success. Now stations were being required to pay more for the privilege of airing it, although such rates can vary for the same show from market to market. Even more significantly, however, *Variety* reported that ad rates for the show were being increased 40 percent for the new season, and that advertisers were purchasing the slots with alacrity. It was a given in the business that the most popular shows could charge the highest advertising rates, and Rosie's show had a lot of younger adult viewers whom advertisers particularly wanted to reach. On top of that, the entire advertising world had sat up and taken notice of what the Listerine "Kiss Rosie" stunt had done for the sales of that long quiescent mouthwash product. Rosie obviously had a special kind of clout with consumers—as Kmart had long since discovered with its Rosie O'Donnell/Penny Marshall ads.

When the fall season opened, Rosie continued much as before along her merry path. Some viewers felt that she had toned down the kid-oriented aspects of the show, and many were just as happy about that, feeling that there had been too much of it. She continued to showcase her love of old television shows, but found some new wrinkles. A viewer from Long Island wrote in that she knew just as much about

Mary Tyler Moore as Rosie did, and maybe more. Rosie, remembering the Mary Tyler Moore trivia game she had played on movie sets, invited her challenger on to the show, and set up podiums as though they were on *Jeopardy.* To Rosie's mock horror, she lost the game when the bets escalated and she placed too much on a tricky question. The audience loved it, and soon the two contestants were duking it out on the new version of *The People's Court,* starring former New York City Mayor Ed Koch as the judge.

The show was running smoothly, and gaining modestly in the ratings, mostly at the expense of *Live with Regis and Kathie Lee,* and the atmosphere on the set seemed as relaxed and bubbly as ever. But behind the scenes a considerable drama was taking place. Rosie had adopted a second child, a daughter, and was keeping the fact a secret even from her co-workers.

Rosie had said many times that she wanted to adopt more children. However, she had said at least as many times that she did not expect to adopt another child until Parker had turned three or entered kindergarten. Clearly, she doted on Parker. While she had, as promised, kept him out of the public eye—the rare magazine photos, as in the February 1997 issue of *Ladies' Home Journal,* always presented him with his back to the camera—she talked about him a great deal. She didn't make him a constant subject, as Kathie Lee Gifford had of her son Cody, and several days might go by without her mentioning him. But she did bring him up sometimes, usually to kid herself about worrying too much about him. And she knew how to get a laugh about having a child. Reading a letter on the air that asked her why she had picked daytime for her show, she replied, "Well, I'm up, you're up, the baby's up. What the hell?"

In magazine interviews and appearances on other television shows she did talk about Parker a lot, however. It was impossible not to, since interviewers always had a question about him. When Mim Udovitch showed up at Rosie's Upper West Side apartment to interview her, she discovered that Rosie's legs had Magic Marker doodles on them. Rosie explained. "My son loves to do tattoos, we do them. And yesterday, at a WNBA game, a two-year-old baby was there and he was crying, so I sat him on my lap and we did tattoos. It doesn't come off for a couple of days." To *Good Housekeeping* she revealed, "We play hide-and-seek around the house. He's exceptionally good at hiding, which is a little scary. I find him inside cabinets—the ones with kidproof locks. He knows how to get them off. We also go to the park and play basketball—we have a tiny little basketball hoop."

But she also said, "I think fame is a very difficult thing for an adult to deal with, and it's nearly impossible for a child to understand. *He* didn't choose a career in showbiz, *I* did. I don't think he should suffer because of that. So, yes, I do worry." She told *Good Housekeeping* that in an interview published in June 1997. It was clearly something that she continued to worry about. On November 11, 1997, she was interviewed on *Access Hollywood*. When Pat O'Brien asked her about having more children, maybe even a "whole bathtub full," she replied that that might be nice, mentioning as always how much her own four siblings meant to her. Then she went on to say, "I'd also like to have someone to share his reality. I think it's going to be weird, having me as a mother, fame, and all that. I think it would be great to have somebody in the bottom bunk so he can lean over and say, 'Doesn't it stink?' " She then acted out in kid talk a conversation between Parker and his possible sibling complaining about Mommy getting all the attention when they went out.

. . .

I love having a sister and brothers, and I don't want to deny Parker that. But we have such a great rapport and routine now. I wonder if having another child will change Parker's personality. He's so great. I think, "Will the next kid be as great? Will I love the next baby as much?" My sister told me you grow a new heart with every child. I think I'm going to wait until Parker is three.

Rosie O'Donnell in *Parade*, July 1997

. . .

What only a very few of those closest to Rosie knew was that the occupant of the imaginary lower bunk was a very real little girl whom Rosie had adopted two months earlier. She had kept the adoption a secret, she would explain, because she wanted the new baby to get settled in before her existence was revealed. But only two days after the *Access*

Hollywood interview was aired, Rosie finally spilled the beans. She announced to her viewers that she had a new baby daughter named Chelsea Belle O'Donnell. "She's beautiful," Rosie said. "It's a very big blessing."

The reason Rosie had chosen this particular day to reveal the truth was that she was to appear on *The View*, the new interview program hosted by Barbara Walters, Meridith Vieira, Star Jones, and Debbie Matenopoulos, immediately afterward. (Both shows were taped on the twelfth, and aired on the thirteenth.) Rosie knew that Naomi Judd was also going to be appearing on *The View* to promote her new book. That presented a problem because Rosie had lied to Judd backstage at her own show the day before. Judd had presented Rosie with two gifts, one for Parker, a toy hammer, the other for Rosie herself. Rosie's gift was a nightlight in the shape of an angel holding a baby. Taken aback, Rosie had blurted out, "How did you know?"

As Judd subsequently told *People,* Rosie had a strange look on her face when she asked this question. "I said, 'What?' " Judd recalled, "And she said, 'I'm getting a little girl.' I said, 'Rosie, I'm delighted for you. When?' She took a beat and then said, 'Uh, uh . . . December.' " Judd also reported that Rosie looked uncomfortable. And she was. Knowing she would be seeing Naomi Judd again the next day at the taping with Barbara Walters, and that Walters herself was likely to ask about Rosie adopting another child, it seemed necessary to reveal the truth. Keeping a secret by not talking about it was one thing, but telling lies in answer to direct questions was another.

On *The View* Rosie revealed that her sister Maureen had suggested the name Chelsea, and that because Rosie wanted Parker to have a hand in naming his sister, she selected Belle, the name of the heroine in his beloved Disney animated feature *Sleeping Beauty.* She also noted that Maureen had told her that Rosie's plan to keep Chelsea Belle a secret until after Thanksgiving was impossible, saying, "You'll never be able to do it. You have a big mouth, you've always had a big mouth."

In fact, Rosie had done remarkably well at keeping her mouth shut. Chelsea Belle had been at Rosie's Nyack, New York, home since September 20, a few days after she was born. Rosie noted that Parker himself had almost given the game away at the studio when he told people, "I have a new baby sister." Taking advantage of a two-and-a-half-year-old's lack of diction, Rosie had quickly said, "No, he has a new baby *sitter."* Baby sister, Rosie revealed, had green eyes like her brother, and was totally bald. "A cutie-patootie," Rosie added, of course.

The new addition to Rosie's family apparently meant that she would not be doing the movie of the musical *Chicago* with Madonna and Goldie Hawn. This was the one film Rosie had indicated she would really like to make, if the timing was right. But while the role of the prison matron in this show seemed very good, it was clear that Rosie's children would come first. Her show was booming along in its second full year, and there was already the nursery at the studio used by Parker and other staff children. In due time his sister would join him there. That there might be further additions to the family could only be a matter of speculation, but it seemed more likely than ever that Rosie had not just been making idle conversation when she said that she would like to have several children. She hadn't even waited until Parker was three to adopt another child. On the other hand, to judge by her conversation with Pat O'Brien, this new addition had been made in part for Parker's own sake, to give him someone to confer with "bunk to bunk" who wasn't famous like his mother.

TWELVE

A Visit from Barbra

The show of shows for Rosie, with Barbra Streisand as her guest, was taped on Wednesday, the nineteenth of November 1997, two days before it would be shown. It was taped ahead of time largely to allay Streisand's basic aversion to live interview shows; if something was said that she regretted, it could be edited out. Rosie herself was not in this case at all averse to taping the show ahead of time. She knew that she would be very nervous, and it was entirely possible that it might be necessary to edit the result because of something she did or failed to do. Advance taping was a safety valve for both Rosie and Barbra.

There was, of course, a live audience for the taping, as always. It would be a terrific audience, since its members would count themselves extremely lucky to have chosen this date to be part of Rosie's show. Only the very first show and the appearance of Tom Cruise could compare as special milestones in the history of *The Rosie O'Donnell Show* up till now; in future anyone in the audience would be able to boast, "I was there when Streisand was on!" To point up the importance of the occasion, the audience member chosen to open the show was none other than Rosie's younger sister, Maureen. With a big smile, Maureen said, "I'm Maureen O'Donnell and this is my sister's show. And this is the one she's been waiting thirty-five years for!"

All dolled up in a white silk pants suit, Rosie entered to a particularly strenuous applause from the excited audience, and then began her usual give-and-take with the person chosen to introduce her, but this time with a special twist.

"Hello," said Rosie. "What was your name again?"

"Maureen."

"Maureen, you look so familiar. You were in that bedroom with me, weren't you?" The giggles of the audience suggested that they had caught on to the taunt to the tabloids that Rosie had made by referring to the well-known fact that she and Maureen had shared a bedroom when they were growing up.

She then asked Maureen to tell people why she was there.

"I'm here to keep you calm," Maureen replied, and added, "If she faints, it's my show."

"No chance of that," said Rosie in her tough-girl manner. "Now sit down and shut up."

Rosie then chatted with John "McD," who said, "I'm so excited for you." But Rosie hardly needed anyone to be excited for her. She held up one collector's item after another, from album covers to refrigerator magnets, mimicked herself singing

"Second Hand Rose" to her mother in the kitchen when she was in the second grade, and got in a joke about her mother's Irish cooking in the process. After holding up the magnets, Rosie said, "Did you notice my hands are shaking?" After the laugh, she insisted, "I'm fine, I *am* fine," to renewed comic effect. Noting that at this point she usually talked about her day, she revealed that she'd been having diarrhea, a fact that perhaps only Rosie O'Donnell could successfully turn into a comic grace note. All in all, her monologue was a prime example of her ability to turn genuine emotion into a stand-up riff, the humor developing out of the realness of the material, while at the same time drawing on the audiences' affectionate complicity in her true nervousness.

A beautifully put-together two-and-a-half-minute montage of Steisand movie and concert clips, with Barbra singing "The Way We Were" in the background, was then shown before going to the commercials. The use of clips of the guests on *The Rosie O'Donnell Show* had always been a cut above what was usually seen on talk shows, but this tribute to a very special guest was as well done as anything done on award shows; no expense had been spared to make this a unique show.

After the commercials, it was time for Streisand's entrance, not from stage right but through the rear curtain used for musical groups. As she appeared, in a formal, long-sleeved but off-the-shoulder black top and silky black slacks, Rosie, standing in front of her desk, burst into tears. "I knew I would do this," she said as she embraced Streisand, who held her close and patted her back. As Rosie's tears continued to stream down, Barbra cupped Rosie's face briefly in her hands. When she was able to speak, Rosie said, "I have to tell you, a little self-indulgently, that in many ways it feels to me like my mom walking through the curtain." Barbra protested that Rosie was going to make her cry, and Rosie said she was sorry and didn't want to upset her in any way, but ". . . you were a constant source of light in an often dark childhood, and you inspired me and gave me the courage to dream of a life better than the one I knew, and I am profoundly grateful to you in so many ways."

. . .

When my mom died, my father took a lot of her stuff out of our house. One of the only things that he left were Barbra Streisand albums, Happening in Central Park, Color Me Barbra, My Name Is Barbra. And that was the only connection that I had to my mom. So when my dad was at work, I used to listen to my Barbra Streisand records and, like, it was really, emotionally for me, reminiscent of my mother. So I've had opportunities to meet her before and I've always sort of avoided it 'cause I thought it will be a little overwhelming.

Rosie O'Donnell, 1996

. . .

It is doubtful that viewers of talk shows sitting at home around the country had been treated to anything this moving since Johnny Carson's final *Tonight Show* guest, Bette Midler, had made him cry by singing "One for My Baby and One More for the Road" to him—and winning an Emmy for her appearance.

But there was still forty minutes of air time for Rosie to get through with the guest she had begged to join her since the inception of the show. And while the emotional high of these early moments was not repeated, the show went remarkably quickly and easily, especially considering the famous interview reticence of the legendary guest and the nervousness of the host. Barbra Streisand appeared more relaxed and less wary than she ever had in such circumstances. She clearly not only trusted Rosie but admired her, noting at one point, "Nothing you do is rude," and playing along in very good-humored amusement with Rosie's encyclopedic knowledge of her career. "You probably know more about me than I do," Barbra said at the outset, and Rosie proceeded to demonstrate, as always, that she knew a very great deal indeed. More than once, Rosie brought up things that she had been told about Barbra—causing the guest to look wary—but her information proved to be correct, something that any world-famous person finds both surprising and gratifying, since people so often get things wrong or repeat false stories.

Rosie noted that Barbra opened on Broadway for the first time in *I Can Get It for You Wholesale* the day after Rosie herself was born. This show, which starred Elliott Gould, whom Barbra would marry, and Lillian Roth, had not been a hit; it ran only a few months, but it had given Streisand a single show-stopping number, "Miss Marmelstein," which she sang while zooming around the stage in a typist's chair. Rosie mother had seen Barbra in the musical, and Rosie still had the program. The fact that Rosie had been born the day before the show opened caused Barbra to murmur, "You're so old?" Rosie hastily replied that it was a matter of Barbra having been so young in her first Broadway show.

Streisand was remarkably forthright in talking to Rosie about stage fright. She recalled that when she appeared on Judy Garland's TV show (a legendary event in television history during which Ethel Merman came up out of the audience to join Judy and Barbra), Garland's hands had been icy cold because she was so frightened. "I wasn't frightened when I was twenty-one," Barbra told Rosie. "I'm more frightened now. There's more to live up to. How do I fulfill your fantasy?" Barbra noted that when she started doing concerts it was frightening because you can't control things the way you can in a studio recording. She also said that that had changed, that in a way she had come to cherish the "flaws" in a live performance for their reality. "There's no such thing as perfection," she said. To which Rosie replied, "But you come very close," which brought a strong applause from the audience.

Rosie asked Barbra if she had ever missed a performance during the Broadway run of *Funny Girl*. Streisand then told how once she had three wisdom teeth removed, but didn't miss that performance; woke up another day with a scratched cornea but didn't miss that performance because her stepfather, who'd never seen her perform, was attending that night. Finally, with a 104-degree temperature and "total laryngitis" she did miss one performance. Rosie wanted to know if Lainie Kazan, her understudy, had gone on for her, and when Barbra said yes, Rosie exclaimed, "She sat here and told me she never went on," referring to one of Lainie Kazan's appearances on Rosie's show. Barbra said that Lainie had even called the press to alert them, to which Rosie chuckled, "Of course, that's Lainie, isn't it?"

At times Rosie and Barbra were playful with each other. Barbra said, "I dieted for you," meaning for this appearance. Rosie replied, "I had diarrhea." Barbra nodded sagely and said, "That's a great way to diet." But there was also serious discussions of *Yentl* and the difficulties of being a female director in Hollywood. Rosie pointed out that Streisand had been the first woman ever to win a Golden Globe award for directing for that film; Streisand seemed surprised that she had been the first, and made it clear that her feelings were still hurt for not getting an Oscar nomination for directing the movie.

On a particularly serious note, the two women discussed breast cancer, a major medical cause for both of them, and one to which they have both devoted their great charitable clout. Barbra explained how she got the idea for her new album *Higher Ground* (which, Rosie pointed out to applause, had gone straight to number one on the pop album chart), when she attended the funeral of her dear friend Virginia Kelly (President Clinton's mother), who had died from breast cancer. Barbra recalled that a girl at the funeral had sung "On Holy Ground" and that "the music just united everyone in their love for this wonderful woman." Barbra had been so moved that she decided to do an album of music that she found inspirational in the same way, and dedicated it to Virginia Kelly.

In the last segment of the show, Rosie brought on James Brolin, the actor who had become central to Streisand's life in recent months. Brolin had had a long career, stretching back to *Marcus Welby, M.D.* on television. Despite good movie roles in such successes as *Von Ryan's Express* (1965), and *Westworld* (1973), his movie career had never really taken off, and while he had appeared in many television movies, he had also moved on to producing and, most recently, directing. After Rosie had introduced the handsome, gray-haired actor as a "cutie-patootie," Brolin came on the set from the usual guest's entrance at stage right, embraced Rosie, and kissed Barbra. "It makes me all warm to see you like that, smooching on my show," Rosie said.

Brolin had been on the show on his own recently, but Rosie had still managed to come up with one of her famous "memory lane" surprises, playing a song from Brolin's 1972 record album, *James Brolin Sings.* Brolin wondered where they had found it, since the most he could say for its success was that it had been number one in the 98¢ bin, and Rosie, laughing, said that she thought that was about where they'd dug it up. Rosie drew the couple out about their first date—a blind date which they had agreed to without knowing much about one another: Barbra, as Rosie brought out, had never seen him on *Marcus Welby,* and he had never seen *Funny Girl,* despite the fact that it had been a big hit that had brought Streisand a Best Actress Oscar in a tie with Katharine Hepburn in *The Lion in Winter*. Rosie suggested that if she had been there at the restaurant that first night she could have filled them both in on each other's careers.

Streisand, known for being reticent in talking about her private life, seemed extraordinarily open in discussing her relationship with Brolin, and he was, too. Rosie tried but failed to get a wedding date out of them. They would only say, "Soon," which led Rosie to relay the information that she had a hiatus in February.

After a commercial break, Rosie made a point of telling her viewers that Streisand had given more than $23 million to charity over the years, and Barbra returned the compliment by citing Rosie's own extensive work for charity. Rosie then presented Barbra with an antique doll for her well-known collection. Barbra seemed genuinely thrilled and touched by the lovely (and very expensive) present. The show concluded with Rosie toasting Streisand and Brolin on their forthcoming marriage. Rosie opened an iced bottle of champagne right at her desk, and poured three glasses. Barbra asked if she had any peach juice, and Rosie, giggling, chided herself for forgetting that Streisand loved that combination, which is known as a Bellini.

But if Rosie had forgotten the peach juice, she had neglected nothing else in attempting to make Barbra feel at home. In fact, as Liz Smith was to reveal later in her column, the rearrangement of the show's set, which Rosie had had carried out a few days earlier, had really been done for Streisand. Rosie had earlier announced that she was going to put the guest seating to her left instead of her right because she was tired of walking all the way back around her desk after coming out to greet her guests. But as Smith noted, Streisand did not like to be filmed from her left side. She was not the first star to favor one profile; Claudette Colbert, who won the Best Actress Oscar for *It Happened One Night* (1934), had required whole sets to be built so that she could enter the scene with her chosen profile toward the camera. Rosie, unbidden, had seen to it that her set was changed for Streisand. As of the next few weeks, however, Rosie had still not changed the set back to its original configuration.

It was also reported that after viewing the tape of her visit, Streisand had wanted one change made. She and Rosie had had a discussion about putting fake biographical notes in the Broadway *Playbill,* a practice its editors frowned upon. In her original bio for *I Can Get It for You Wholesale,* Barbra—as Rosie had noticed—said that she was born in Rangoon and raised in Madagascar. On the show, Rosie asked where Rangoon was, and Barbra answered "near Africa." This would have been correct for Madigascar, the island nation off Africa's east coast, but it was incorrect for Rangoon, which is the capital of Burma. Barbra was embarrassed by the mistake and asked if it could be edited out. While Rosie said that could be done, it would also leave an obvious gap, leading viewers to speculate exactly what had been taken out, and would also disrupt the flow of the conversation. Barbra accepted this argument, saying much for her graciousness. The fact that Rosie chose to debate the issue rather than agree immediately to remove the offending moment, said a great deal about her. There was no one she admired more than Barbra Streisand, and no one, including Tom Cruise, whom she had more deeply wanted on her show. By standing up to Streisand on this point, Rosie demonstrated how much in command of her show, her career, and her life she was.

Twenty-four years earlier, when her mother Roseann died, the ten-year-old daughter who bore the same name, had turned to her mother's Barbra Streisand albums for solace in a stricken home. The little girl, that devoted fan, had grown up to become a star in her own right, one of the most popular people in show business. The long climb from comedy clubs that at first had barely let her in the door was over. She was a national figure with fans who numbered in the millions. And among those fans, somewhere, there was undoubtedly a little girl with problems who wanted to be a star someday, a little girl for whom Rosie O'Donnell was now the "source of light," the shining beacon who illuminated life's possibilities. And it is abundantly clear that few things could give Rosie O'Donnell greater satisfaction than to be that source of light.